Nurses

Nurses at the Front

*Writing the Wounds of
the Great War*

EDITED BY MARGARET R. HIGONNET

NORTHEASTERN UNIVERSITY PRESS
BOSTON

Title page photograph: Mairi Chisholm, 1917 (Q2966),
courtesy of the Imperial War Museum, London

The Backwash of War by Ellen N. La Motte was originally published in
1916 by G. P. Putnam's Sons, New York. *The Forbidden Zone* by Mary Borden was
originally published in 1929 by Heinemann, London, and in 1930 by Doubleday,
Doran, New York. The excerpts from *The Forbidden Zone* are copyright 1929, 1930
by Doubleday, a division of Bantam Doubleday
Dell Publishing Group. Used by permission of Doubleday,
a division of Random House, Inc.

Library of Congress Cataloging-in-Publication Data

Nurses at the Front : writing the wounds of the Great War /
edited by Margaret R. Higonnet.
p. cm.
An anthology of reprinted war sketches from E. N. La Motte's
"The backwash of war" and M. Borden's "The forbidden zone."
Includes bibliographical references.
ISBN 1-55553-484-8 (pbk. : alk. paper)—ISBN 1-55553-485-6 (alk. paper)
1. La Motte, Ellen Newbold, 1873–1961. 2. Borden, Mary. 3. World War,
1914–1918—Personal narratives, American. 4. World War, 1914–1918—Medical
care—Western Front. 5. Nurses—United States—Biography.
I. Higonnet, Margaret R. II. La Motte, Ellen Newbold, 1873–1961.
Backwash of war. III. Borden, Mary. Forbidden zone.
D640.A2 N87 2001
940.4'7573'092—dc21   2001018013

Designed by Ann Twombly
Composed in Fairfield by Wellington Graphics, Westwood, Massachusetts.
Printed and bound by Edwards Brothers, Inc., Lillington, North Carolina.
The paper is EB Natural, an acid-free stock.

MANUFACTURED IN THE UNITED STATES OF AMERICA

05 04 03 02 01   5 4 3 2 1

Contents

❧

Contents

Introduction

❧

Ellen Newbold La Motte (1873–1961)
and Mary Borden (1886–1968)

IT WAS THE WAR that had taken me to France," recollected
the novelist and poet Mary Borden.[1] At the very moment
when advancing armies were driving refugee women and
children away from their homes in the battle zones of Belgium
and Poland, the Great War was drawing other women toward
the line of fire. In the early days of the war, a desire to serve
where the need was greatest rallied women of all ages and from
many countries who were "as eager to get to the Front as any
Boy."[2]

But how to get to the front? Bureaucratic red tape slowed
the passage of eager women to the war zone. The American
Margaret Hall wrote from Paris despairingly, "I have no hopes
of getting anywhere near the front. The Red Cross does not
send women near."[3] Military regulations, social prohibitions,
and political resistance all impeded women's efforts, until several years of catastrophic losses made the mobilization of
womanpower necessary. Nonetheless, old and young lined up
to volunteer in almost any capacity—as hospital orderlies, as
canteen workers ladling soup at railroad stations, or as clerks
tracking those missing in action.

Women who wanted not only to serve their country but also

to do so near the front found nursing the most acceptable channel for their energies. When pointless interviews and delays proved frustrating, as Vera Brittain testified, determined women such as Dr. Elsie Inglis of the Scottish Women's Hospitals and Mrs. St. Clair Stobart formed their own units comprising women surgeons, nurses, drivers, radiologists, and administrators, and departed for Belgium, France, or the Balkans.

Even though the United States was thousands of miles away, unaffected by the flood of refugees, and remained neutral, not joining the Allies in declaring war on Germany until May 1917, a surprising number of American women—perhaps 25,000— volunteered to help the war effort in Europe.[4] Margaret Deland, a canteen worker, believed that American women's combination of personal freedom and experience in volunteer work had shaped "a little army of girls" that could not be held back.[5] At the outbreak of the war some happened to be already in Europe; others went over on their own, defying official resistance in 1914–15 to women's participation. For the most part these volunteers were educated, middle-class, and highly motivated. Some even left children and other dependents behind.[6]

This collection presents the wartime sketches of two exceptional Americans who went to nurse in Europe, and who met at the Western Front. Mary Borden, a Vassar graduate married to an Englishman, Captain George Douglas Turner, was an aspiring writer, a mother, and a fashionable hostess in avantgarde London circles in 1914. When she signed up with the

French Red Cross, she had never nursed before. Ellen La Motte, the older of the two, was a professional nurse with administrative experience, a specialist in tuberculosis from Baltimore.

The war called La Motte to France in November 1914: "I had come over from New York in response to a cable from a friend in Paris, to whom I had written asking if there was any work that I could do."[7] The American hospital in Paris where she began was equipped with an ironically wasteful surplus that made her restless to move to a hospital closer to the battlefields. She wanted a job where her skills would matter. By contrast, when Mary Borden volunteered in 1914, she found herself assigned to a typhoid hospital outside Dunkirk that lacked feeding cups, urinals, and bedpans. She too felt her efforts were being squandered. La Motte and Borden both make palpable their desire not only for personal and national liberation, but for control over the meaning of their work.

Perhaps inspired in part by other women's medical units that had been set up under French control, the wealthy Borden within a few months of her arrival in France decided to establish her own frontline surgical unit under French military command in the Belgian zone. Almost immediately, La Motte joined that frontline unit. From this professional partnership between the nurse and the future novelist, with their complementary ways of seeing, sprang two of the most powerful books of testimony about nursing at the front to emerge from the Great War.

Introduction

We know surprisingly little about these two women, especially when compared to the mythic aura that surrounds a much-decorated pair of British heroines at the front, Elsie Knocker and Mairi Chisholm, who began their volunteer work in the fall of 1914 as ambulance drivers, then set up an emergency station in the ruined Belgian town of Pervyse. The pair from Pervyse became famous for the first aid they gave to the wounded, whom they carried from the nearby battlefields on their own backs; their work was publicized by journalists such as the American Mary Roberts Rinehart, and their story was retold in fund-raising efforts.

No such publicity marked the collaboration of La Motte and Borden at Hôpital Chirurgical Mobile No. 1. We must therefore piece together details of their wartime careers from sketches they published in the war years and later. La Motte published one story in 1916, "Heroes," which she collected the same year with her unpublished sketches in *The Backwash of War*. Borden appears to have written prose fragments as well as the poems she published in the *English Review* during the war; she did not publish the fragments or the episodes she later recorded until *The Forbidden Zone* appeared in 1929, juxtaposing prose and poetry. There are striking parallels between the two collections: specific shocking incidents, unconventional types of patients, and taboo themes such as hypocrisy and ambition. There is a particularly telling similarity in the bitter irony with which the two women describe what they saw during their frontline nursing. Moreover, the two collections are related through their recurrent portrayals of two anonymous nurses who appear to be stylized images of La Motte and Borden themselves. The most important piece of evidence linking the two, however, comes from a few lines by Gertrude Stein, who may have sent the cable that called La Motte to Paris.

A 1902 graduate of the Johns Hopkins Training School, Ellen La Motte was a nurse of growing distinction in Baltimore when she met Gertrude Stein (who failed in her medical studies at Johns Hopkins before she moved on to Paris to become a writer).[8] La Motte renewed contact with Stein when she volunteered her medical skills and knowledge of epidemiology at a Paris hospital. A proud descendant of French Huguenots, she was eager in 1914 to get to France or to Serbia (where Inglis and St. Clair Stobart had sent women's units). As she self-mockingly recalled in an article she wrote in 1915, she had gone over with an idealistic if naïve desire for "service on the battlefield, gathering in the wounded on stretchers and conveying them to a waiting ambulance."[9]

The thread of La Motte's war work is picked up briefly in Stein's *Autobiography of Alice B. Toklas*. With characteristic repetitions for emphasis, Stein explains:

Ellen La Motte and Emily Chadbourne, who had not gone to Servia, were still in Paris. Ellen La Motte, who was an ex Johns Hopkins nurse, wanted to nurse near the front. She was still gun shy but she did want to nurse at the front, and they met Mary Borden-Turner who was running a hospital at the front and Ellen La Motte did for a few months nurse at the front.[10]

Stein's incantatory stress on frontline service underscores how emphatically the front defined the concept of war experience for women as well as for men. She confirms that it was of particular importance to La Motte to serve where there was the greatest need, an impetus she shared with younger women such as Vera Brittain. As one might expect in Stein's tribute to her own relationship with Alice Toklas, she also three times insists on La Motte's partnership with Emily Chadbourne, who accompanied her to France, then worked with La Motte during the next decade to suppress the opium trade in China.[11]

While in France from 1914 to 1916, La Motte wrote several articles about her experiences as a nurse and a civilian observer, which were published back home for an American public hungry for firsthand accounts about the war. As a United States citizen and therefore a "neutral," La Motte was doubtless freer to judge the war effort than a British or a French national such as May Sinclair or Colette would have been.[12] Yet her critique is surprisingly incisive. Most journalistic accounts of hospital work, such as those by Mary Roberts Rinehart for the *Saturday Evening Post,* were uncritical propaganda. La Motte's first essay, devoted to her 1914 initiation into war work in a Paris hospital (probably the American Hospital at Neuilly, run by Amy Vanderbilt), criticizes dilettantes who are contributing token time and effort to hospital tasks, doctors who squander scarce supplies, and administrators who misallocate resources to treat minor cases at the rear rather than the severe casualties at the front. Society girls who are gathering "experiences which will tell well in next year's ball-rooms," she implies, translate the soldiers' accounts of war into mere chit-chat.[13] La Motte stands out as well among journalists for her complex narrative strategies. Her article alternates between an "I" who stands back and judges her coworkers, and a "we" that concedes her potential complicity, as a writer herself, with the story-seeking socialites. This use of "we" in turn invites her readers to reflect on their own involvement in the culture of war. We can see the same sophisticated techniques in the sketches she published a year later.

Within months of her arrival in Paris, La Motte transferred to Borden's newly established mobile surgical unit in the war zone near Ypres. Two autobiographical articles for the *Atlantic Monthly* from this period reconsider the symbolic separation of the civilian zone from the militarized zone, so often identified with the distinction between women's sphere and men's sphere. The first article depicts her arrival in the port town of Dunkirk just as it comes under fire from long-range German cannon. As an eyewitness, she records the menacingly random disappearance of buildings, the relentless rhythms of terror, and the agitation of the townspeople, who have become the spectators of their own fate.[14] The second article describes an outing with another nurse from Borden's hospital who is looking for a relative at a nearby camp; the "gun shy" La Motte decides not to go all the way to the entrenchments, but finds herself nonetheless exposed to more German shelling than her friend, who has driven up to the front positions in the "forbidden zone"—a phrase that later became the title of Mary Borden's book.[15]

Introduction

By 1916 La Motte's sketches about her work at the front had appeared under the troubling title *The Backwash of War*; their datelines suggest that she composed most of them in three bursts of inspiration, in April 1915, December 1915, and May to June 1916, during trips back to Paris. Stein, who noted that La Motte was a diverting storyteller and had "collected a set of souvenirs of the war for her cousin Dupont de Nemours," did not mention the volume in the *Autobiography*.[16] The sketches in *The Backwash of War* are not, in any case, diverting souvenirs. Unlike many wartime medical reminiscences that collect sentimentalized portraits of wounded soldiers, these pages were not token bits abstracted for propagandistic or nostalgic purposes.

As her Introduction declares, the focus is on the "backwash," or ugliness, churned up in the wake of war. Indeed, the book was so frank and powerful that it could not be distributed in England or France. By 1918, with American troops finally going over to France, the U.S. government inked out advertisements for the book in the *Liberator*, a monthly on whose editorial board La Motte was serving. This censorship is not surprising: her detached fragments form a harshly realistic image of men's wounds and the conditions under which military medicine was practiced. Even more important, the fragments build a moral indictment of those who were making decisions about the lives and deaths of men. La Motte depicts the war itself as a trauma, a medical image mirrored in the ironic fragments by Mary Borden in *The Forbidden Zone*, published thirteen years later.

Introduction

Once La Motte's book was complete, probably in the summer of 1916, she decided to leave for China. Unfortunately,
Stein's *Autobiography* offers no further information either
about how La Motte had met Borden or about why she left.
But in her enigmatic third-person voice, Stein does explain her
social acquaintance with Borden, as a "millionaire" from Chi-
cago, whose hospitality was welcome in a time of war short-
ages.

> She [Borden] was very enthusiastic about the work of Ger-
> trude Stein and traveled with what she had of it and volumes
> of Flaubert to and from the front. She had taken a house near
> the Bois and it was heated and during that winter when the
> rest of us had no coal it was very pleasant going to dinner
> there and being warm.[17]

Borden's own autobiography, *Journey Down a Blind Alley*
(1946), offers a few more glimpses of how she came to France.
In the radiant summer of 1914, this cosmopolitan twenty-eight
year old had been entertaining the avant-garde writers Ford
Madox Ford and Wyndham Lewis in Scotland. (Lewis later recalled Borden as an "attractive American" who stood out from
"bogus society" by her classless "freshness."[18]) When word
came of the war, she left her children behind in England in order to nurse typhoid patients in a former casino at Malo-les-
Bains, near Dunkirk, on the northern French coast. She then
applied to General Joffre for authorization to create a surgical
hospital of her own at the front. She staffed it with her own se-

lection of British and American nurses, while the French Army provided a French *médecin chef* (chief medical officer), surgeons, N.C.O.'s, and orderlies. Her wealth permitted her to equip the hundred-bed hospital, and her willpower enabled her to keep it going for the duration of the war. Although previously untrained, Borden learned to administer injections and to assist at operations: "My nurses told me what to do and I did it to the best of my ability." Her autobiography recalls a level of exhaustion that made her into "a sleepwalker, an automaton."[19] As the army was pushed back, her mobile unit moved from near Poperinghe and Ypres in Belgium to the Somme in France, where she met her second husband, Captain Edward Spears.[20] She won British medals and the French Croix de Guerre for her war work, and she was named a member of the French Legion of Honor.

Like La Motte, Borden began to compose her sketches and poetry in brief lulls in the fighting between 1914 and 1918. Some of her poetry on the Battle of the Somme appeared in the *English Review* in 1917; new stories were added to the collection when it was published under the title *The Forbidden Zone* in 1929. Her Preface explains that the sketches are "fragments of a great confusion" whose apparently unbearable plainness actually softens the reality. These pictures inescapably blur "the bare horror of facts" because part of the truth "can never be written."

The prose sketches by the two women are closely linked in their content and form. Several portray two nurses who appear to correspond to La Motte and Borden themselves. In La

Introduction

Motte's "A Belgian Civilian," for example, the nurse-narrator describes the administrative director of the hospital, that is, Borden: "The *Directrice* of this French field hospital was an American, by marriage a British subject, and . . . had three children of her own whom she had left in England." *Madame la Directrice* (who first appears in an uncollected sketch, "A Joy Ride"), becomes an emblem of the nurse's idealized purity, as well as a representative of the medical hierarchy ("Heroes").[21] At times she is concerned primarily with building the reputation of her hospital ("A Citation"). At other times the *Directrice* is concerned with emotional rather than physical care ("A Belgian Civilian"); her sentimental concerns are contrasted to the professionalism of the night nurse (identified with La Motte's narrator).

From the other side of the looking glass, Borden's nurse-narrator compares her own sensitivity to the calm of a highly disciplined nurse on the ward ("Rosa"). Perhaps modeled on La Motte, the professional night nurse is less emotional than the narrator, and under the stress of continuous emergency service she may even reach a dehumanized numbness that Borden's narrator dreads for herself ("Moonlight"). These double portraits in both collections suggest at once mutual respect and an ambivalence in the relationship between La Motte and Borden. They also reflect a larger artistic strategy of splitting the nurse into two figures, in order to explore the dilemmas faced in frontline nursing, where self-control and technical efficiency conflict with emotional involvement and the threat of hysteria.

Introduction

Not only do we find the nurse split into a pair, like a diptych, but in both collections we find the narrator mentally divided. La Motte's narrative position is particularly unstable and elusive. In her opening sketch, "Heroes," the narrator first seems to align herself with the military doctor's notion of honor, with military discipline, and with the "joy" of caring for severely wounded war heroes. Halfway through, however, she shifts to an alignment with the third-person indirect discourse of a "night nurse" who begins to question herself and to doubt the cult of heroism. Like Diogenes with his lamp, a seeker of truth bearing her candle, she lets the men for whom she cares have the last word. Similarly, in a sketch about military medals, "Pour la Patrie," La Motte opens with a sardonic comparison between the relentless routines of war medicine and the variegated practice of peacetime medicine in a city hospital: "the hospitals of peace time are not nearly so stupid, so monotonous, as the hospitals of war." Here again, she turns to an individual dying soldier for her final comment. Shot "as usual" in the abdomen, awarded a perfunctory medal that seems a "cheap" exchange for his life, the patient suddenly confesses that his heroism had been forced: "My Captain won it for me. . . . He had a revolver in his hand." La Motte's narrative voice thus shifts from a mocking dialogue with the reader to an unadorned, shocking realism.

In a different register, Borden makes use of the distance between the time of composition and that of the experience, in order to expose similar splits between first person and third person in her narrator's mind. Thus the retrospective sketch

Introduction

"Blind" contrasts the nurse's past involvement to her present search for meaning: "Looking back, I do not understand that woman—myself—standing in that confused goods yard filled with bundles of broken human flesh. . . . I think that woman, myself, must have been in a trance, or under some horrid spell." This grammatical self-division is a strategy she echoes in her autobiography. By multiplying perspectives, these writers ask the reader to weigh the competing values engaged in the practice of military medicine.

La Motte and Borden both portray narrators who struggle to understand the war as they play down their own roles and abilities. Sometimes a narrator directly exhorts the reader to enter into the intense world she describes: "Come, I'll show you" ("Belgium"). The world that Borden and La Motte are so eager for civilians to see is a harsh one, with the wind blowing the tin roof off the hut where the wounded lie, water dripping onto beds, surgical wards crowded with the living, the dead, and the bodily remnants of both. Their narrators call upon the reader to challenge the conditions created by war, conditions that, as they constantly remind us, are economic: anesthetic at so many francs a can, gauze at so many dollars a roll, a "victory" at so many men a yard. The ultimate form of an economic mindset is the basic medical practice of triage at the front, in which neither those who will surely survive nor those who cannot be saved will be treated immediately. Only the other third, those whose survival depends upon immediate treatment, are the ones that the mobile hospital can afford to spend time on. Any distraction—a dying ten-year-old boy, or a fatal case of gas gangrene—represents a potential sacrifice of other lives that might be saved. Borden compares the night nurse who steels herself to her task, like a "machine," to an officer passing in the night who is "calculating the number of men needed to repair yesterday's damage, and the number of sandbags required to repair their ditches" ("Moonlight").

Writing in the voice of the nurse enables La Motte and Borden to engage the central theme of the Great War: needless wounding and destruction. Their portraits of individual soldiers explicitly depict the mangled bodies and the damaged spirits that made this war into a world catastrophe. Men's bodies are atomized: they are reduced to the locus of the wound when they are assigned to an operating table or a ward: heads, knees, abdomens. Part of a brain comes off in a bandage; an "errant eye" dislodged from its socket must be bound back into place.

What their critical perspective brings to this theme is the argument that nursing must be a kind of resistance to the physical and spiritual destruction wrought by war. This thesis is certainly not just a literal one about the power of bodily healing. The much-touted miracle of plastic surgery, a medical specialty that emerged during the war, is shown by La Motte to leave a grotesquely reconstructed knob in place of a nose carved out by a shell ("A Surgical Triumph"). Until we change our basic premises, the wizardry of surgeons will be subordinate to and often defeated by the art of warfare; nurses will be faced with what Borden calls "miserable futility" ("Enfant de Malheur"). She lets us understand that the nurse's show of being busy, "making an unnecessary fuss over my duties," is a form of symbolic resistance to the presence of inexorable death ("Enfant de Malheur," "Paraphernalia"). Yet even in combat against death, the nurse conspires with a military system that will send those she heals back to the front "to be torn again and mangled." For the hospital itself ironically participates in the social organization of death: "it is all arranged" ("Conspiracy").

Because these two nurses hope to enable the reader's resistance to propaganda and understanding of war as a social trauma, the issue of truth is central to their work. Although La Motte maintains in her 1934 Introduction that her sketches "could apply equally well to any other hospital back of the lines," she also declares, "They are true."[22] In "Women and Wives" the narrator likewise explains, "There are many people to write you of the noble side, the heroic side, the exalted side of war. I must write you of what I have seen, the other side, the backwash. They are both true." According to Borden as well, "I have not invented anything in this book." Borden's 1929 Preface to her volume claims that five stories were "written recently from memory; they recount true episodes that I cannot forget." It seems clear that at least some of these incidents were witnessed by La Motte, who was the first to set them down.

The most remarkable parallel between the two collections emerges from the juxtaposition of Borden's "Rosa," one of those "true episodes," and La Motte's "Heroes." Each sketch describes the arrival of an attempted suicide. In the operating room, the narrator learns from the doctor that their task is to heal the self-inflicted wound, so that the patient can then be court-martialed: "he must be nursed back to health, until he was well enough to be stood up against a wall and shot" ("Heroes"). In all likelihood an actual case of suicide aroused these two writers' consciences, as they nursed side by side, because it so explicitly summed up the ethical dilemmas of military medicine. From the military point of view, such soldiers had to be executed as examples to deter attempts to escape service; it was feared that panic and despair might be communicable. Military hospitals preoccupied with detecting faked wounds suppressed suicide reports. From the nurse's point of view, the primary obligation (symbolized by the Hippocratic oath) was to save lives. To heal men so that they can go back into the trenches to kill or be killed, La Motte ironically observes, is "a dead-end occupation." For Borden, the key mystery is the motive of the soldier, which might have been personal despair in response to the loss of "Rosa," whose name he calls, rather than cowardice. She rebels against "your military regulations asking me to save him for you so that you can shoot him." Both narrators sum up the contradiction: "This is War." By exposing the violence that rules the day, La Motte and Borden encourage readers to resist propaganda and to question complacent fantasies about the healing professions in wartime.

A second striking parallel involves the character study of the "Apache," or hoodlum, in La Motte's "A Citation" and Borden's "Enfant de Malheur," another one of the "true episodes" she added a decade after the war. Both sketches portray a youth from the underworld of Paris who has done penal service in the colonies with the "Bataillons d'Afrique"; called up to serve with shock troops at the front, the Apache comes into the hospital mortally wounded. It is this unlikely character who attracts attention because of his unrewarded heroism, his fierce resistance to death, and his gentle endurance of pain. Under the harsh light of the operating table, the petty thief comes to seem like a social victim of rich capitalists, political imperialists, and ambitious doctors who try out a succession of experimental techniques on his body. By joining wartime heroism to everyday criminality this figure enables the two writers to ask who is a hero, and what is socially acceptable violence.

More general parallels concern the way these two nurses depict the place of women in wartime. Women are not exempt from their satiric vision. The sketches criticize civilians, including women, who continue to pursue private gain in the marketplace; they attack hypocrisy and private ambition among medical staff of both sexes. These writers have little patience with "curious, sensation hunting" Americans "who had remained in Paris to see the war, or as much of it as they could, in order to enrich their own personal experience" ("A Surgical Triumph"). La Motte mocks the pragmatism and greed of a Belgian mother who wants to hasten back to her profitable bar serving soldiers, rather than comfort her wounded boy or remain for his funeral. She reminds us that women remain in the "forbidden zone," working to survive by all available means; there is no clear alignment of men with war and women with peace. La Motte sardonically contrasts soldiers' fond remembrance of their wives with their casual use of local women as sexual objects, some of them just fourteen years old ("Women and Wives"). As a form of economic exploitation, she suggests, prostitution collapses the moral distinctions between "us" and "them," between "good" and "bad" women. She forces us to reconsider whether Belgian women who serve German soldiers differ in any way from those who serve the French, and to ask in turn what are the conditions that produce prostitution.

Even more shockingly, Borden links the destruction of men's bodies to their literal emasculation, a taboo topic that permits her to ask whether war also evacuates women's sexuality: "there are no men here, so why should I be a woman?" ("Moonlight"). This dramatic break with the mythic sexualization of nurses' intimate contact with men's bodies contrasts with a man's novel such as *A Farewell to Arms*, where the nurse's role is to care sexually and emotionally for the wounded soldier.

The new medical technologies, such as X rays, enabled medical observers to penetrate men's bodies, exploring deep into those bodies for hidden shrapnel and damaged organs, in order to heal them. The clinical gaze of the experienced nurse also can become an art that discerns the truth at a glance, like the touch that instantly palpates depths and penetrates the truth.[23] While doctors and nurses may thus know the physical condition of the wounded, they may not know other kinds of secrets that men carry from the front. When a man's eye has been destroyed, does he see something beyond what other men see? With one dying eye a man may look back at the hell of the trenches, with the other he may peer forward into death. Blindness and insight become inverted. Medical staff may in fact have to inure themselves to what they observe in order to continue to function effectively. As Borden writes about the night nurse, "She is blind so that she cannot see the torn parts of men she must handle." The tellers of these stories call upon the reader to come "see the wounded" and to gain knowledge about the war ("Moonlight"). Yet the stories also question whether there can be a complete vision of war that would correspond to the unified map drawn by officialdom.[24]

IN THE INITIAL REVIEWS and again in the recent revival of interest in women's writings about the Great War, La Motte's and Borden's writings provoked sharp debates concerning not only what is represented but how it is represented. Some early readers found these depictions of military medicine unacceptably "revolting—even sickening at times."[25] Thus, in 1916, one reviewer complains that La Motte has reached "the limit of realism," because she "perceives nothing but what is debased in human weakness and suffering."[26] Another instead praises her because she "exhibits with painful frankness the septic, gangrenous aspects of war, which are, after all, just as true as its inspiring, red-blooded side."[27] Even eighteen years later, when the volume was reprinted, the *Saturday Review of Literature* found some of the episodes, which "have the air of having happened just as they are told," to be "almost unbearably horrible."[28] By 1934, however, reviewers tended to agree with La Motte's claim that her work had been suppressed by U.S. censors in 1918 precisely because of its honesty. One wrote: "It is easy to understand why these stories by an American nurse were suppressed during the war. They describe far too truthfully for the interests of war propagandists the human wreckage that was carried off the battlefield into the squalor of a French field hospital."[29]

In the thirties, general agreement about what a war book should look like led most readers to acknowledge the power of La Motte's depiction, which they identified with her ironic narrative voice. The *Christian Century* wittily praised the "perfect art" of these sketches: "She sees and tells with the meticulous precision of a Tolstoy, plus a certain grim humor and a gentle irony which probably saved her sanity and certainly saved her style."[30] The great books about war now sprang to mind, not only Tolstoy but Erich Maria Remarque: "As writing they hold their own beside *All Quiet on the Western Front*, or whatever may be taken as the best representative of the bestiality of war."[31] Like the *Saturday Review of Literature*, which noted La Motte's simplicity, economy, and "savage irony," the *New Republic* praised La Motte's "laconic irony" and "stark realism," comparing her work to Henri Barbusse's landmark war novel, *Under Fire* (1916).[32]

Even though Borden's work appeared after Remarque's, however, it confronted in 1929–30 the same sort of shocked responses that had greeted La Motte's work in 1916. Her acutely observed details provoked revulsion from one reviewer, who condemned them as "almost inconceivably horrible."[33] The *Times Literary Supplement* reported a similar queasiness in its

Introduction

reviewer: "The scenes inside the operating room during a battle are dreadful, and all the more so because they are described
with considerable power. . . . There is some risk that the fash-
ion in which the subject is handled will make it appear that the
hospital was for the wounded a place of horror rather than
of relief."[34] Another reviewer accused Borden of "breaches of
good taste" in the "ghoulish" sketch entitled "Blind," and
condemned a "graphic" dramatic sketch, "In the Operating
Room," as "far too intense, too unsparing."[35] Such readers pre-
ferred her whimsical, "charming" descriptions of towns and
motor cars deformed by the stresses and destructiveness of
war.[36]

At the same time, Borden's self-conscious style, which em-
phasizes imagery such as moonlight and allegorizes "Pain," led
reviewers to debate whether it was too artistic. While one critic
felt "the fictional disguise is obviously very slight,"[37] another
saw a marriage of truth with art: "Nothing is invented, and yet
it is evident that a vivid imagination has taken hold of the material, pulled it into shape and made of it a vehicle for indignation, bewilderment, and a kind of frozen horror. The sketches
and little stories are not direct transcriptions from reality, but
bits of art."[38] That imaginative shaping was precisely the prob-
lem for some readers. It led the *Saturday Review of Literature*,
for example, to damn Borden for the same transformation:
"With a poet's gift of rhythm, beauty, and feeling, Miss Borden
has taken the rawest materials of life and turned them into a
work of art. But what price art?"[39] This reviewer has summed
up the prevailing attitude toward war writing: it is antithetical

to any fiction whatsoever. To craft the raw material of war, to fictionalize, is to contaminate the evidence and to abandon authenticity.

Obviously, such reviewers believed in the possibility of "direct transcriptions from reality" that would be entirely opposed to artistic transformation. Modern theories of history have moved beyond this simplistic view of the writing of war, since any recording of experience passes through the filters of language and narrative, through what Hayden White calls "emplotment."[40] The familiar distinction between factual and fictional prose has been blurred by literary critics who view different types of autobiographical prose, such as journalism, diary, memoir, and sketch, as parts of a continuum, in all of which we find choices of narrative perspective, genre, or metaphor. Readers have become more aware of the ways in which any author selects a narrative voice to enter into a dialogue with the reader.

Feminist theories of life-writing have further blurred the lines between these genres of self-representation by setting them in the context of social "scripts."[41] Not only do they question assumptions that experience can be transparently depicted, they also suggest that one's sense of agency may be constricted by social narratives about what women "should" do. In wartime such regulatory concepts have even more force for both men and women, as La Motte and Borden were fully aware. The sense of a self, which we so often take for granted, is not stable or coherent through time, especially when an intense propaganda effort is under way to reshape women's sense of their own capacities. We can understand a letter, a diary, a memoir, or a *testimonio* not just as a sincere act of self-expression but as a many-voiced act of self-presentation whose self varies according to the intended audience. In this theoretical context, the internal division of the narrators as well as the doubling of the nurse figure in these two writers becomes highly suggestive.

Different testimonial forms can be intricately interrelated. To compare the historical value of a diary with that of a memoir, it is helpful to keep in mind that distance in time may blur some details, while other suppressed, traumatic memories may return. To cite one of the best-known writers of World War I, Vera Brittain in her memoir, *Testament of Youth* (1934), depicts a younger self significantly different from the Vera in the diary she kept during the war, *Chronicle of Youth*; Brittain in 1934 was not only remembering the past but writing for the present and a possible future. Similarly, Virginia Woolf, who mined the observations and images of her diaries to compose her fiction, hoped later to smelt their "loose, drifting material" into the ingot of a memoir. Borden too kept diaries from which she later composed her autobiography; they may also have served as the loose material from which she filtered her fictional fragments. Moreover, the paired nurses in the sketches by La Motte and Borden suggest that these two women were writing a dialogue with each other, as well as a record for themselves and an appeal to the public.

These questions about identity and historical narrative can help us become aware of the ways in which a narrator performs a succession of roles, momentarily conforming to patriotic prejudices, for example, before shifting to another stance. We can hear changing intonations such as irony, rising hysteria, or blasphemy. Nonetheless, modern feminist critics have not agreed about the persona and voice of the narrators in the sketches by Borden and La Motte. Some readers interpret the repetitious descriptive language as an expression of survivor's guilt, or as a flight from reality. Sandra Gilbert, for example, has maintained that Borden expresses "culpable numbness" through her depiction of the nurse as "no longer a woman . . . really dead, past resurrection."[42] In a similar vein, Dorothy Goldman describes Borden's writing as "uncomprehending, neurasthenic," and finds a deliberate insistence on "dissociating herself from the unbearable reality."[43] Such a judgment invites comparison to Jane Marcus's argument that memoirs about nursing tend to deploy an "anaesthetic esthetic." For Marcus, there are two kinds of nurses' texts, exemplified by Helen Z. Smith's *Not So Quiet . . .* and by Borden's *Forbidden Zone*: the first marks wounds through an aesthetic of textual fragmentation (with ellipses and other breaks), while the second aims to heal the scars inflicted by wartime observations by "choosing to numb consciousness." Marcus also indicates the unstable genre of the sketches by La Motte and Borden, which she calls "memoirs," proposing that they "deserve particular mention because of the brilliance of the writing as well as historical documentation."[44]

We may note that narrative voice in these sketches is not

only a choice, as Marcus says, but a staging of possible attitudes. Shifting perspectives on the war can pry the reader free from received opinions. Thus, where Sandra Gilbert finds a "dreadful confession," another reader may instead discover irony.[45] Furthermore, the two aesthetics that Marcus describes seem to meet in the work of La Motte and Borden. Writing to expose wounds—whether those of the harshly delineated soldier victims or those of traumatized medical workers—is surely a first step toward healing wounds. Moreover, the stylistic display of the numbing effects of war should not be understood as a denial of wounds, for it constitutes yet another charge in the indictment of war as a trauma experienced by men and women alike.

In listening to these disturbing voices, we should bear in mind that radical stylistic innovations were already under way in the writings of Gertrude Stein and the imagist Amy Lowell, as well as in the prose and poetry of male artists such as Wyndham Lewis, Apollinaire, and e. e. cummings. The hermetically allusive poems and dramatic fragments that Stein penned in this period impress upon us not only her profound rejection of patriarchy but her commitment to breaking up syntax and semantic discipline. Like Picasso's cubist experiments with perspective, her experiments with grammar challenge temporal subordination and unified identity. If Borden did carry Stein's works to the front with her, then we can better understand why she uses a "strikingly modern prose of flat repetition," as Claire Tylee has said, in order to resist the puffery of propaganda.[46] Another possible model was Lowell, who wrote "free verse" prose poems about the war. Lowell's declarative "imagist" sentences flattened perspectives and condensed narrative forms. Thinking about the war not as a cause of artistic innovation but as a moment set within the larger frame of sustained artistic change can thus help us to understand the devices these nurses use to depict the war accurately and forcefully. By setting La Motte and Borden next to these writers, we can expand our definition of a female modernism.[47]

Moving in experimental circles, La Motte and Borden drew on similar tools to break down the uniformity of an official, militarized, propagandistic view of the war. They insert French terms not only to lend an air of authenticity to the text, but also to estrange the scenes described and to create the sense of a special, hallucinatory wartime world, where understanding can be many-layered. They make bitter puns: La Motte, for example, picks up the French term for a disabled soldier who has been discharged, *réformé*, to comment on the grotesque reforming of his body by plastic surgery. Because war kills so swiftly, it is "clean" and "humane," but boring, she suggests, thus satirizing the traditional view that heroic death spares men from slow erosion by disease and suffering. Not only does she undermine the dichotomy between "us" and "them" that governs so much wartime propaganda, she directly exposes the relationship between oppressive discourse and physical violence. In her sketch about the deathbed confession of the dying Apache, she explains: "he was being forced into it. Forced into acceptance. Beaten into submission, beaten into resignation" to the "noble words" of self-sacrifice that rattle "in the stillness like the popping of a *mitrailleuse,*" or machine gun ("Pour la Patrie").

Borden, too, deliberately shocks us by repeating the domestic images of laundry that political and military propagandists were using to justify a war of purification: just as buttons are sewn back onto shirts, so men's bodies are washed and stitched back together until they wear out. The blasphemous nature of war becomes apparent through her parody of liturgical language in a hymn to the omnipresence of ceaseless combat, as "war without end."

Nurses' texts offer a fresh perspective on the canon of war texts—which consists almost entirely of soldiers' texts centered on the experiences of combat, such as being wounded, seeing a comrade blown apart, sharing a trench with exposed bits of men's bodies, and experiencing psychological trauma in the relentless renewal of bombardment. Many readers have concluded that only soldiers who bore the wounds of combat had the authority to write about war. The hallmarks of "modernist" literature in turn corresponded to the symptoms of a soldier's shell shock: ruptured narrative, with embedded flashbacks and ellipses suggestive of erased memory; intense imagery or obscene details suggestive of hypersensitivity; and obsessive repetitions indicative of emotional numbing. For the critic Samuel Hynes, the modernist text depicts "disfigured and fragmented human bodies—all rather small-scale, all randomly disposed,

and all rendered without judgement or expressed emotion"
in a phantasmagorical world where individual things and moments are "equal parts of one chaos." For Hynes, "Writing
like this, seeing like this, . . . divides the soldier from the civilian."[48]

If we turn to the texts by La Motte and Borden, however, we
find that seeing like this, writing like this, joins the nurse and
the soldier. For the traumatizing exposure to the wounded body
was experienced not only by combatants but by noncombat-
ants at the front as well. Although spared the immediate experience of combat, nurses developed a professional understanding of the mutilating consequences of war. The nurse's
testimony takes the form of startling physical details, abrupt
juxtapositions, and the suppression of emotion. The deadpan,
scientifically neutral depiction of the wounded bodies La
Motte and Borden treated constitutes one of their claims to
authority about the war. They lay claim to authority as well
through their symptomatic writing, like that of the shell-
shocked soldier, with its driven pace, hyper-intense images,
repetitions, and fragmentation of the landscape of war into individual sketches.

This writing of the wounds of war is what Borden means
when she explains in her Preface that she presents "fragments
of a great confusion." The results are remarkable. The observed details that are seared into the descriptions in both *The
Backwash of War* and *The Forbidden Zone* testify to the intense
and chaotic medical arena within which La Motte and Borden
fought together to bring down mortality rates. At the same

time, these two nurses succeed in projecting a much larger vision of the war, one that creatively transforms analyses of individual cases into an anatomy of war itself.

MARGARET R. HIGONNET

Notes

1. Mary Borden, *Journey Down a Blind Alley* (New York: Harper & Brothers, 1946), 4–5.

2. Dora M. Walker, *With the Lost Generation, 1915–1919* (Hull: A. Brown, 1970), 1.

3. Margaret Hall, "Letters and Photographs from the Battle Country, 1918–1919," September 1918, Margaret Hall Papers, Massachusetts Historical Society.

4. See Dorothy Schneider and Carl J. Schneider, *Into the Breach: American Women Overseas in World War I* (New York: Viking, 1991), 11, 287–89.

5. Margaret Deland, *Small Things* (New York: Appleton, 1919), 8.

6. The middle-aged settlement worker Edith Holliday reflected in a diary-letter, "I couldn't leave Guy and the children unless some thing very deep and serious called me and as it is, the pull between my longing to be with them all at home and the feeling I must be heart and soul in the cause is constant. . . . I hope when I get there, the push that has carried me along so far will continue till I have been of some real service." After many rebuffs, she joined the Red Cross Canteen Service. Edith Holliday, entry for May 4, 1918, Edith Holliday Papers, Massachusetts Historical Society.

7. Ellen N. La Motte, "An American Nurse in Paris," *Survey* 34 (July 10, 1915), 333.

8. La Motte was Superintendent of the Tuberculosis Division for

the Baltimore Health Department from 1910 to 1913; she innovated social prevention through supervision by visiting nurses. *The Tuberculosis Nurse* (New York: Putnam, 1915).

9. La Motte, "American Nurse," 333.

10. Gertrude Stein, *Autobiography of Alice B. Toklas* (1933; reprint, New York: Vintage, 1970), 170.

11. La Motte won the Lin Tse Hu Memorial Medal (1930) for her work in China against the opium trade, as well as an order of merit from the Japanese Red Cross. See Stein, *Autobiography of Alice B. Toklas,* 158, 169, 170.

12. Not all Americans were so forthright in what they wrote during the war. La Motte's incisive commentary predates by four years the satire by Edith Wharton, "Writing a War Story" (1919).

13. La Motte, "American Nurse," 335.

14. La Motte, "Under Shell-Fire at Dunkirk," *Atlantic Monthly* 116 (November 1915), 692–700.

15. La Motte, "A Joy Ride," *Atlantic Monthly* 118 (October 1916), 482.

16. Stein, *Autobiography of Alice B. Toklas,* 158.

17. Ibid. 170.

18. Lewis, *Blasting and Bombardiering* (London: Eyre & Spottiswood, 1937), 60–61.

19. Borden, *Journey Down a Blind Alley,* 7, 9.

20. She divorced Turner. Spears, who remained in Paris for the peace conference, retired from the army and became a member of Parliament. He returned to serve as major general in World War II, when he was the British mediator with General de Gaulle. Borden returned to France with another medical unit during the "drôle de guerre" before the defeat of France by Germany, then served in the Middle East.

21. A sketch added in 1934, "Esmeralda," depicts a little goat who

knocks down a French general inspecting the hospital with the *Directrice*, and who must therefore be disposed of. This scapegoat may symbolize La Motte's own departure from the hospital following her portrayal of Borden and her attack upon militarized ideology in *The Backwash of War*.

22. Ellen N. La Motte, *The Backwash of War* (New York: Putnam, 1934), vi–vii. The 1934 Introduction explains the suppression of the volume in 1918 as "undesirable," because "true."

23. See Michel Foucault, *The Birth of the Clinic: An Archeology of Medical Perception* (New York: Pantheon, 1973), 121–22.

24. On the wartime visual field, see Jean Gallagher, *The World Wars through the Female Gaze* (Carbondale: Southern Illinois University Press, 1998).

25. *New York Times Book Review,* October 15, 1916, p. 432.

26. *Independent* 88 (November 13, 1916), 284.

27. *Springfield Republican*, October 2, 1916, p. 6.

28. *Saturday Review of Literature* 11 (September 22, 1934), 134.

29. "Book Parade," *Forum* 92 (December 1934), x.

30. *Christian Century*, September 12, 1934, p. 1151.

31. *Saturday Review of Literature* 11 (September 22, 1934), 134.

32. *New Republic* (November 7, 1934), 374.

33. Cyril Falls, *War Books: An Annotated Bibliography of Books about the Great War*. Intro. R. J. Wyatt (London: Greenhill, 1989), 267.

34. *Times Literary Supplement*, December 5, 1929, p. 1030.

35. *Saturday Review of Literature* 7.7 (July 26, 1930), 7.

36. *New Republic* 62 (May 14, 1930), 357.

37. *The Nation & Athenaeum* 46 (January 4, 1930), 489.

38. *Books*, April 13, 1930, p. 24.

39. *Saturday Review of Literature* 7.7 (July 26, 1930), 7.

40. Hayden White, *Metahistory: The Historical Imagination in*

Introduction

Nineteenth-Century Europe (Baltimore: Johns Hopkins University
Press, 1977), and *Figural Realism: Studies in the Mimesis Effect* (Baltimore: Johns Hopkins University Press, 1999).

41. See Sidonie Smith and Julia Watson, Introduction to *Women,
Autobiography, Theory: A Reader*, ed. Smith and Watson (Madison:
University of Wisconsin Press, 1998), 3–52.

42. Sandra Gilbert and Susan Gubar, *No Man's Land: The Place of
the Woman Writer in the Twentieth Century. Vol. 2: Sexchanges* (New
Haven: Yale University Press, 1989), 320.

43. Dorothy Goldman, with Jane Gledhill and Judith Hattaway,
Women Writers and World War I (Boston: Twayne, 1995), 73.

44. Jane Marcus, "The Nurse's Text: Acting Out an Anaesthetic
Aesthetic," Afterword to Irene Rathbone, *We That Were Young* (New
York: Feminist Press, 1989), 477, 469. "Helen Z. Smith" is the pseudo-
nym of Evadne Price.

45. Gilbert and Gubar, *No Man's Land*, 320.

46. Claire Tylee, *The Great War and Women's Consciousness* (London: Macmillan, 1989), 97.

47. See Jane Marcus, "Afterword: Corpus/Corps/Corpse: Writing
the Body In/At War," in Helen Zenna Smith [Evadne Price], *Not So
Quiet . . . Stepdaughters of War* (New York: Feminist Press, 1989),
241–300.

48. Samuel Hynes, *A War Imagined: The First World War and English Culture* (New York: Atheneum, 1991), 115, 116.

Glossary of French Terms

❧

Ah mon Dieu!: Oh Lord!

Amputés: amputees

Apache: street tough, hooligan

Baraques: huts

Bataillon d'Afrique: African battalion

Brancardiers: stretcher bearers

Briquet: cigarette lighter

Casse-croûte: snack

Cela pique! Cela brûle!: It stings! It burns!

C'est triste! C'est bien triste!: It's sad! It's quite sad!

Ces sales Belges!: Those dirty Belgians!

Ces sales Bosches!: Those dirty Germans!

Cité: central registry at the police office on the Ile de la Cité

Croix de Guerre: Military Cross

Damné: damned one

Dieu, notre seul espoir—Dieu, notre Sauveur: O Lord, our sole hope—O Lord, our savior

Dieu qui nous regarde, ayez pitié. Dieu le Sauveur, je vous supplie: O Lord who watcheth over us, have pity upon us. O Lord, our savior, I beseech you

Directrice: directress

Glossary of French Terms

Eau de Javel: bleach
Enfant de Malheur: child of sorrow
En repos: at rest
Entente: allies (literally, agreement or understanding)
Equipes: teams
Estaminet: bar, public house
Fêtes: festivals
Garçon d'hôtel: hotel boy
Gestionnaire: military purveyor
Grands blessés: severely wounded
Infirmier: male nurse, orderly
Je ne meurs pas: I am not dying
Je ne tiens plus: I can't stand it any longer
Je ne voudrais pas mourir: I do not want to die
Jésu—Dieu—Sauveur qui nous regarde: Jesus—Lord God—
   Savior who looks down upon us
Joyeux: light infantry in African battalion, hence "outcast"
Képi: military cap
Librement: freely
Mairies: town halls
Médaille Militaire: Military Medal
Médecin chef: chief medical officer
Médecin Inspecteur: Medical Inspector General
Médecin Major: medical officer
Mitrailleuse: machine gun
Mon ami: my friend
Mon vieux: old chap
Musette: kit

Glossary of French Terms

Obus: shell

Oui: yes

La Patrie: fatherland

Pépères: Territorial soldiers (informal, "old fellows")

Petit parisien: Little Parisian (newspaper)

Piqûres: injections

Poste de secours: emergency station

Pour la Patrie: For the fatherland

Préfecture de Police: police station

Que voulez-vous?: What do you want?

Réformés: disabled, released from service

Le Rire: The Laugh (newspaper)

Sabot: wooden shoe

Salle: ward, room

Salle d'Attente: waiting room

Salle des Grands Blessés: ward for the severely wounded

Trottoir: sidewalk

Vaguemestre: military postal orderly

Valeur et discipline: valor and discipline

Vieux pères: old fathers

Voilà!: There!

The Backwash of War

The Human Wreckage of the Battlefield as Witnessed by an American Hospital Nurse

❧❦❧

ELLEN N. LA MOTTE

Introduction

❧

THIS WAR has been described as "Months of boredom, punctuated by moments of intense fright." The writer of these sketches has experienced many "months of boredom," in a French military field hospital, situated ten kilometres behind the lines, in Belgium. During these months, the lines have not moved, either forward or backward, but have remained dead-locked, in one position. Undoubtedly, up and down the long-reaching kilometres of "Front" there has been action, and "moments of intense fright" have produced glorious deeds of valour, courage, devotion, and nobility. But when there is little or no action, there is a stagnant place, and in a stagnant place there is much ugliness. Much ugliness is churned up in the wake of mighty, moving forces. We are witnessing a phase in the evolution of humanity, a phase called War—and the slow, onward progress stirs up the slime in the shallows, and this is the Backwash of War. It is very ugly. There are many little lives foaming up in the backwash. They are loosened by the sweeping current, and float to the surface, detached from their environment, and one glimpses them, weak, hideous, repellent. After the war, they will consolidate again into the condition called Peace.

The Backwash of War

After this war, there will be many other wars, and in the intervals there will be peace. So it will alternate for many generations. By examining the things cast up in the backwash, we can gauge the progress of humanity. When clean little lives, when clean little souls boil up in the backwash, they will consolidate, after the final war, into a peace that shall endure. But not till then.

E. N. L. M.

Heroes

⚜

WHEN HE COULD STAND IT no longer, he fired a revolver up through the roof of his mouth, but he
made a mess of it. The ball tore out his left eye, and
then lodged somewhere under his skull, so they bundled him
into an ambulance and carried him, cursing and screaming, to
the nearest field hospital. The journey was made in double-
quick time, over rough Belgian roads. To save his life, he must
reach the hospital without delay, and if he was bounced to death
jolting along at breakneck speed, it did not matter. That was
understood. He was a deserter, and discipline must be maintained. Since he had failed in the job, his life must be saved, he
must be nursed back to health, until he was well enough to be
stood up against a wall and shot. This is War. Things like this
also happen in peace time, but not so obviously.

At the hospital, he behaved abominably. The ambulance
men declared that he had tried to throw himself out of the
back of the ambulance, that he had yelled and hurled himself
about, and spat blood all over the floor and blankets—in short,
he was very disagreeable. Upon the operating table, he was no
more reasonable. He shouted and screamed and threw himself
from side to side, and it took a dozen leather straps and four or

five orderlies to hold him in position, so that the surgeon could examine him. During this commotion, his left eye rolled about loosely upon his cheek, and from his bleeding mouth he shot great clots of stagnant blood, caring not where they fell. One fell upon the immaculate white uniform of the Directrice, and stained her, from breast to shoes. It was disgusting. They told him it was *La Directrice,* and that he must be careful. For an instant he stopped his raving, and regarded her fixedly with his remaining eye, then took aim afresh, and again covered her with his coward blood. Truly it was disgusting.

To the *Médecin Major* it was incomprehensible, and he said so. To attempt to kill oneself, when, in these days, it was so easy to die with honour upon the battlefield, was something he could not understand. So the *Médecin Major* stood patiently aside, his arms crossed, his supple fingers pulling the long black hairs on his bare arms, waiting. He had long to wait, for it was difficult to get the man under the anæsthetic. Many cans of ether were used, which went to prove that the patient was a drinking man. Whether he had acquired the habit of hard drink before or since the war could not be ascertained; the war had lasted a year now, and in that time many habits may be formed. As the *Médecin Major* stood there, patiently fingering the hairs on his hairy arms, he calculated the amount of ether that was expended—five cans of ether, at so many francs a can—however, the ether was a donation from America, so it did not matter. Even so, it was wasteful.

At last they said he was ready. He was quiet. During his

struggles, they had broken out two big teeth with the mouth gag, and that added a little more blood to the blood already choking him. Then the *Médecin Major* did a very skilful operation. He trephined the skull, extracted the bullet that had lodged beneath it, and bound back in place that erratic eye. After which the man was sent over to the ward, while the surgeon returned hungrily to his dinner, long overdue.

In the ward, the man was a bad patient. He insisted upon tearing off his bandages, although they told him that this meant bleeding to death. His mind seemed fixed on death. He seemed to want to die, and was thoroughly unreasonable, although quite conscious. All of which meant that he required constant watching and was a perfect nuisance. He was so different from the other patients, who wanted to live. It was a joy to nurse them. This was the *Salle* of the *Grands Blessés,* those most seriously wounded. By expert surgery, by expert nursing, some of these were to be returned to their homes again, *réformés,* mutilated for life, a burden to themselves and to society; others were to be nursed back to health, to a point at which they could again shoulder eighty pounds of marching kit, and be torn to pieces again on the firing line. It was a pleasure to nurse such as these. It called forth all one's skill, all one's humanity. But to nurse back to health a man who was to be court-martialled and shot, truly that seemed a dead-end occupation.

They dressed his wounds every day. Very many yards of gauze were required, with gauze at so many francs a bolt. Very much ether, very much iodoform, very many bandages—it was an expensive business, considering. All this waste for a man who was to be shot, as soon as he was well enough. How much better to expend this upon the hopeless cripples, or those who were to face death again in the trenches.

The night nurse was given to reflection. One night, about midnight, she took her candle and went down the ward, reflecting. Ten beds on the right hand side, ten beds on the left hand side, all full. How pitiful they were, these little soldiers, asleep. How irritating they were, these little soldiers, awake. Yet how sternly they contrasted with the man who had attempted suicide. Yet did they contrast, after all? Were they finer, nobler, than he? The night nurse, given to reflection, continued her rounds.

In bed number two, on the right, lay Alexandre, asleep. He had received the *Médaille Militaire* for bravery. He was better now, and that day had asked the *Médecin Major* for permission to smoke. The *Médecin Major* had refused, saying that it would disturb the other patients. Yet after the doctor had gone, Alexandre had produced a cigarette and lighted it, defying them all from behind his *Médaille Militaire*. The patient in the next bed had become violently nauseated in consequence, yet Alexandre had smoked on, secure in his *Médaille Militaire*. How much honour lay in that?

Here lay Félix, asleep. Poor, querulous, feeble-minded Félix, with a foul fistula, which filled the whole ward with its odour. In one sleeping hand lay his little round mirror, in the other, he clutched his comb. With daylight, he would trim and comb his moustache, his poor, little drooping moustache, and twirl the ends of it.

Beyond lay Alphonse, drugged with morphia, after an intolerable day. That morning he had received a package from home, a dozen pears. He had eaten them all, one after the other, though his companions in the beds adjacent looked on with hungry, longing eyes. He offered not one, to either side of him. After his gorge, he had become violently ill, and demanded the basin in which to unload his surcharged stomach.

Here lay Hippolyte, who for eight months had jerked on the bar of a captive balloon, until appendicitis had sent him into hospital. He was not ill, and his dirty jokes filled the ward, provoking laughter, even from dying Marius. How filthy had been his jokes—how they had been matched and beaten by the jokes of others. How filthy they all were, when they talked with each other, shouting down the length of the ward.

Wherein lay the difference? Was it not all a dead-end occupation, nursing back to health men to be patched up and returned to the trenches, or a man to be patched up, court-martialled and shot? The difference lay in the Ideal.

One had no ideals. The others had ideals, and fought for them. Yet had they? Poor selfish Alexandre, poor vain Félix, poor gluttonous Alphonse, poor filthy Hippolyte—was it possible that each cherished ideals, hidden beneath? Courageous dreams of freedom and patriotism? Yet if so, how could such beliefs fail to influence their daily lives? Could one cherish standards so noble, yet be himself so ignoble, so petty, so commonplace?

The Backwash of War

At this point her candle burned out, so the night nurse took another one, and passed from bed to bed. It was very incomprehensible. Poor, whining Félix, poor whining Alphonse, poor whining Hippolyte, poor whining Alexandre—all fighting for *La Patrie*. And against them the man who had tried to desert *La Patrie*.

So the night nurse continued her rounds, up and down the ward, reflecting. And suddenly she saw that these ideals were imposed from without—that they were compulsory. That left to themselves, Félix, and Hippolyte, and Alexandre, and Alphonse would have had no ideals. Somewhere, higher up, a handful of men had been able to impose upon Alphonse, and Hippolyte, and Félix, and Alexandre, and thousands like them, a state of mind which was not in them, of themselves. Base metal, gilded. And they were all harnessed to a great car, a Juggernaut, ponderous and crushing, upon which was enthroned Mammon, or the Goddess of Liberty, or Reason, as you like. Nothing further was demanded of them than their collective physical strength—just to tug the car forward, to cut a wide swath, to leave behind a broad path along which could follow, at some later date, the hordes of Progress and Civilization. Individual nobility was superfluous. All the Idealists demanded was physical endurance from the mass.

Dawn filtered in through the little square windows of the ward. Two of the patients rolled on their sides, that they might talk to one another. In the silence of early morning their voices rang clear.

Heroes

"Dost thou know, *mon ami*, that when we captured that German battery a few days ago, we found the gunners chained to their guns?"

PARIS
18 December, 1915

Alone

❧

ROCHARD DIED TO-DAY. He had gas gangrene. His thigh, from knee to buttock, was torn out by a piece of German shell. It was an interesting case, because the infection had developed so quickly. He had been placed under treatment immediately too, reaching the hospital from the trenches about six hours after he had been wounded. To have a thigh torn off, and to reach first-class surgical care within six hours, is practically immediately. Still, gas gangrene had developed, which showed that the Germans were using very poisonous shells. At that field hospital there had been established a surgical school, to which young men, just graduated from medical schools, or old men, graduated long ago from medical schools, were sent to learn how to take care of the wounded. After they had received a two months' experience in this sort of war surgery, they were to be placed in other hospitals, where they could do the work themselves. So all those young men who did not know much, and all those old men who had never known much, and had forgotten most of that, were up here at this field hospital, learning. This had to be done, because there were not enough good doctors to go round, so in order to care for the wounded at all, it was necessary to furbish up the immature and the senile. However, the *Médecin Chef* in charge of the hospital and in charge of the surgical school, was a brilliant surgeon and a good administrator, so he taught the students a good deal. Therefore, when Rochard came into the operating room, all the young students and the old students crowded round to see the case. It was all torn away, the flesh from that right thigh, from knee to buttock, down to the bone, and the stench was awful. The various students came forward and timidly pressed the upper part of the thigh, the remaining part, all that remained of it, with their fingers, and little crackling noises came forth, like bubbles. Gas gangrene. Very easy to diagnose. Also the bacteriologist from another hospital in the region happened to be present, and he made a culture of the material discharged from the wound, and afterwards told the *Médecin Chef* that it was positively and absolutely gas gangrene. But the *Médecin Chef* had already taught the students that gas gangrene may be recognized by the crackling and the smell, and the fact that the patient, as a rule, dies pretty soon.

They could not operate on Rochard and amputate his leg, as they wanted to do. The infection was so high, into the hip, it could not be done. Moreover, Rochard had a fractured skull as well. Another piece of shell had pierced his ear, and broken into his brain, and lodged there. Either wound would have been fatal, but it was the gas gangrene in his torn-out thigh that would kill him first. The wound stank. It was foul. The *Médecin Chef* took a curette, a little scoop, and scooped away the dead flesh, the dead muscles, the dead nerves, the dead blood-vessels. And so many blood-vessels being dead, being scooped away by that sharp curette, how could the blood circulate in the top half of that flaccid thigh? It couldn't. Afterwards, into the deep, yawning wound, they put many compresses of gauze, soaked in carbolic acid, which acid burned deep into the germs of the gas gangrene, and killed them, and killed much good tissue besides. Then they covered the burning, smoking gauze with absorbent cotton, then with clean, neat bandages, after which they called the stretcher bearers, and Rochard was carried from the operating table back to the ward.

The night nurse reported next morning that he had passed a night of agony.

"Cela pique! Cela brule!" he cried all night, and turned from side to side to find relief. Sometimes he lay on his good side; sometimes he lay on his bad side, and the night nurse turned him from side to side, according to his fancy, because she knew that on neither one side nor the other would he find relief, except such mental relief as he got by turning. She sent one of the orderlies, Fouquet, for the *Médecin Chef*, and the *Médecin Chef* came to the ward, and looked at Rochard, and ordered the night nurse to give him morphia, and again morphia, as often as she thought best. For only death could bring relief from such pain as that, and only morphia, a little in advance of death, could bring partial relief.

So the night nurse took care of Rochard all that night, and turned him and turned him, from one side to the other, and

gave him morphia, as the *Médecin Chef* had ordered. She listened to his cries all night, for the morphia brought him no relief. Morphia gives a little relief, at times, from the pain of life,
but it is only death that brings absolute relief.

When the day nurse came on duty next morning, there was
Rochard in agony. *"Cela pique! Cela brule!"* he cried. And
again and again, all the time, *"Cela pique! Cela brule!"*, meaning the pain in his leg. And because of the piece of shell, which
had penetrated his ear and lodged in his brain somewhere, his
wits were wandering. No one can be fully conscious with an
inch of German shell in his skull. And there was a full inch of
German shell in Rochard's skull, in his brain somewhere, for
the radiographist said so. He was a wonderful radiographist
and anatomist, and he worked accurately with a beautiful, expensive machine, given him, or given the field hospital, by
Madame Curie.

So all night Rochard screamed in agony, and turned and
twisted, first on the hip that was there, and then on the hip
that was gone, and on neither side, even with many ampoules
of morphia, could he find relief. Which shows that morphia,
good as it is, is not as good as death. So when the day nurse
came on in the morning, there was Rochard strong after a
night of agony, strong after many *picqures* of strychnia, which
kept his heart beating and his lungs breathing, strong after
many *picqures* of morphia which did not relieve his pain. Thus
the science of healing stood baffled before the science of destroying.

Alone

Rochard died slowly. He stopped struggling. He gave up trying to find relief by lying upon the hip that was there, or the hip that was gone. He ceased to cry. His brain, in which was lodged a piece of German shell, seemed to reason, to become reasonable, with break of day. The evening before, after his return from the operating room, he had been decorated with the *Médaille Militaire,* conferred upon him, *in extremis,* by the General of the region. Upon one side of the medal, which was pinned to the wall at the head of the bed, were the words: *Valeur et Discipline.* Discipline had triumphed. He was very good and quiet now, very obedient and disciplined, and no longer disturbed the ward with his moanings.

Little Rochard! Little man, gardener by trade, aged thirty-nine, widower, with one child! The piece of shell in his skull had made one eye blind. There had been a hæmorrhage into the eyeball which was all red and sunken, and the eyelid would not close over it, so the red eye stared and stared into space. And the other eye drooped and drooped, and the white showed, and the eyelid drooped till nothing but the white showed, and that showed that he was dying. But the blind, red eye stared beyond. It stared fixedly, unwinkingly, into space. So always the nurse watched the dull, white eye, which showed the approach of death.

No one in the ward was fond of Rochard. He had been there only a few hours. He meant nothing to any one there. He was a dying man, in a field hospital, that was all. Little stranger Rochard, with one blind, red eye that stared into Hell, the Hell he had come from. And one white, dying eye, that showed his hold on life, his brief, short hold. The nurse cared for him very gently, very conscientiously, very skilfully. The surgeon came many times to look at him, but he had done for him all that could be done, so each time he turned away with a shrug. Fouquet, the young orderly, stood at the foot of the bed, his feet far apart, his hands on his hips, and regarded Rochard, and said: *"Ah! La la! La la!"* And Simon, the other orderly, also stood at the foot of the bed, from time to time, and regarded Rochard, and said: *"Ah! C'est triste! C'est bien triste!"*

So Rochard died, a stranger among strangers. And there were many people there to wait upon him, but there was no one there to love him. There was no one there to see beyond the horror of the red, blind eye, of the dull, white eye, of the vile, gangrene smell. And it seemed as if the red, staring eye was looking for something the hospital could not give. And it seemed as if the white, glazed eye was indifferent to everything the hospital could give. And all about him was the vile gangrene smell, which made an aura about him, and shut him into himself, very completely. And there was nobody to love him, to forget about that smell.

He sank into a stupor about ten o'clock in the morning, and was unconscious from then till the time the nurse went to lunch. She went to lunch reluctantly, but it is necessary to eat. She instructed Fouquet, the orderly, to watch Rochard carefully, and to call her if there was any change.

After a short time she came back from lunch, and hurried to see Rochard, hurried behind the flamboyant, red, cheerful

Alone

screens that shut him off from the rest of the ward. Rochard was dead.

At the other end of the ward sat the two orderlies, drinking wine.

PARIS
April 15, 1916.

A Belgian Civilian

A BIG ENGLISH AMBULANCE drove along the high road from Ypres, going in the direction of a French field hospital, some ten miles from Ypres. Ordinarily, it could have had no business with this French hospital, since all English wounded are conveyed back to their own bases, therefore an exceptional case must have determined its route. It was an exceptional case—for the patient lying quietly within its yawning body, sheltered by its brown canvas wings, was not an English soldier, but only a small Belgian boy, a civilian, and Belgian civilians belong neither to the French nor English services. It is true that there was a hospital for Belgian civilians at the English base at Hazebrouck, and it would have seemed reasonable to have taken the patient there, but it was more reasonable to dump him at this French hospital, which was nearer. Not from any humanitarian motives, but just to get rid of him the sooner. In war, civilians are cheap things at best, and an immature civilian, Belgian at that, is very cheap. So the heavy English ambulance churned its way up a muddy hill, mashed through much mud at the entrance gates of the hospital, and crunched to a halt on the cinders before the *Salle d'Attente*, where it discharged its burden and drove off again.

{ 21 }

The Backwash of War

The surgeon of the French hospital said: "What have we to do with this?" yet he regarded the patient thoughtfully. It was a very small patient. Moreover, the big English ambulance had driven off again, so there was no appeal. The small patient had been deposited upon one of the beds in the *Salle d'Attente,* and the French surgeon looked at him and wondered what he should do. The patient, now that he was here, belonged as much to the French field hospital as to any other, and as the big English ambulance from Ypres had driven off again, there was not much use in protesting. The French surgeon was annoyed and irritated. It was a characteristic English trick, he thought, this getting other people to do their work. Why could they not have taken the child to one of their own hospitals, since he had been wounded in their lines, or else have taken him to the hospital provided for Belgian civilians, where, full as it was, there was always room for people as small as this. The surgeon worked himself up into quite a temper. There is one thing about members of the *Entente*—they understand each other. The French surgeon's thoughts travelled round and round in an irritated circle, and always came back to the fact that the English ambulance had gone, and here lay the patient, and something must be done. So he stood considering.

A Belgian civilian, aged ten. Or thereabouts. Shot through the abdomen, or thereabouts. And dying, obviously. As usual, the surgeon pulled and twisted the long, black hairs on his hairy, bare arms, while he considered what he should do. He considered for five minutes, and then ordered the child to the operating room, and scrubbed and scrubbed his hands and his hairy arms, preparatory to a major operation. For the Belgian civilian, aged ten, had been shot through the abdomen by a German shell, or piece of shell, and there was nothing to do but try to remove it. It was a hopeless case, anyhow. The child would die without an operation, or he would die during the operation, or he would die after the operation. The French surgeon scrubbed his hands viciously, for he was still greatly incensed over the English authorities who had placed the case in his hands and then gone away again. They should have taken him to one of the English bases, St. Omer, or Hazebrouck—it was an imposition to have dumped him so unceremoniously here simply because "here" was so many kilometres nearer. "Shirking," the surgeon called it, and was much incensed.

After a most searching operation, the Belgian civilian was sent over to the ward, to live or die as circumstances determined. As soon as he came out of ether, he began to bawl for his mother. Being ten years of age, he was unreasonable, and bawled for her incessantly and could not be pacified. The patients were greatly annoyed by this disturbance, and there was indignation that the welfare and comfort of useful soldiers should be interfered with by the whims of a futile and useless civilian, a Belgian child at that. The nurse of that ward also made a fool of herself over this civilian, giving him far more attention than she had ever bestowed upon a soldier. She was sentimental, and his little age appealed to her—her sense of proportion and standard of values were all wrong. The *Directrice* appeared in the ward and tried to comfort the civilian, to still his howls, and then, after an hour of vain effort, she de-

cided that his mother must be sent for. He was obviously dying, and it was necessary to send for his mother, whom alone of
all the world he seemed to need. So a French ambulance,
which had nothing to do with Belgian civilians, nor with Ypres,
was sent over to Ypres late in the evening to fetch this mother
for whom the Belgian civilian, aged ten, bawled so persistently.

She arrived finally, and, it appeared, reluctantly. About ten
o'clock in the evening she arrived, and the moment she
alighted from the big ambulance sent to fetch her, she began
complaining. She had complained all the way over, said the
chauffeur. She climbed down backward from the front seat,
perched for a moment on the hub, while one heavy leg, with
foot shod in slipping *sabot,* groped wildly for the ground. A soldier with a lantern watched impassively, watched her solid
splash into a mud puddle that might have been avoided. So she
continued her complaints. She had been dragged away from
her husband, from her other children, and she seemed to have
little interest in her son, the Belgian civilian, said to be dying.
However, now that she was here, now that she had come all
this way, she would go in to see him for a moment, since the
Directrice seemed to think it so important. The *Directrice* of
this French field hospital was an American, by marriage a British subject, and she had curious, antiquated ideas. She seemed
to feel that a mother's place was with her child, if that child
was dying. The *Directrice* had three children of her own whom
she had left in England over a year ago, when she came out to
Flanders for the life and adventures of the Front. But she

would have returned to England immediately, without an instant's hesitation, had she received word that one of these children was dying. Which was a point of view opposed to that of this Belgian mother, who seemed to feel that her place was back in Ypres, in her home, with her husband and other children. In fact, this Belgian mother had been rudely dragged away from her home, from her family, from certain duties that she seemed to think important. So she complained bitterly, and went into the ward most reluctantly, to see her son, said to be dying.

She saw her son, and kissed him, and then asked to be sent back to Ypres. The *Directrice* explained that the child would not live through the night. The Belgian mother accepted this statement, but again asked to be sent back to Ypres. The *Directrice* again assured the Belgian mother that her son would not live through the night, and asked her to spend the night with him in the ward, to assist at his passing. The Belgian woman protested.

"If *Madame la Directrice* commands, if she insists, then I must assuredly obey. I have come all this distance because she commanded me, and if she insists that I spend the night at this place, then I must do so. Only if she does not insist, then I prefer to return to my home, to my other children at Ypres."

However, the *Directrice,* who had a strong sense of a mother's duty to the dying, commanded and insisted, and the Belgian woman gave way. She sat by her son all night, listening to his ravings and bawlings, and was with him when he died, at three o'clock in the morning. After which time, she requested to be taken back to Ypres. She was moved by the death of her son, but her duty lay at home. *Madame la Directrice* had promised to have a mass said at the burial of the child, which promise having been given, the woman saw no necessity for remaining.

"My husband," she explained, "has a little *estaminet,* just outside of Ypres. We have been very fortunate. Only yesterday, of all the long days of the war, of the many days of bombardment, did a shell fall into our kitchen, wounding our son, as you have seen. But we have other children to consider, to provide for. And my husband is making much money at present, selling drink to the English soldiers. I must return to assist him."

So the Belgian civilian was buried in the cemetery of the French soldiers, but many hours before this took place, the mother of the civilian had departed for Ypres. The chauffeur of the ambulance which was to convey her back to Ypres turned very white when given his orders. Everyone dreaded Ypres, and the dangers of Ypres. It was the place of death. Only the Belgian woman, whose husband kept an *estaminet,* and made much money selling drink to the English soldiers, did not dread it. She and her husband were making much money out of the war, money which would give their children a start in life. When the ambulance was ready she climbed into it with alacrity, although with a feeling of gratitude because the *Directrice* had promised a mass for her dead child.

A Belgian Civilian

"These Belgians!" said a French soldier. "How prosperous they will be after the war! How much money they will make from the Americans, and from the others who come to see the ruins!"

And as an afterthought, in an undertone, he added: *"Ces sales Belges!"*

The Interval

❧

AS AN ORDERLY, Erard wasn't much good. He never waited upon the patients if he could help it, and when he couldn't help it, he was so disagreeable that they wished they had not asked him for things. The newcomers, who had been in the hospital only a few days, used to think he was deaf, since he failed to hear their requests, and they did not like to yell at him, out of consideration for their comrades in the adjoining beds. Nor was he a success at sweeping the ward, since he did it with the broom in one hand and a copy of the *Petit Parisien* in the other—in fact, when he sat down on a bed away at the end and frankly gave himself up to a two-year-old copy of *Le Rire,* sent out with a lot of old magazines for the patients, he was no less effective than when he sulkily worked. There was just one thing he liked and did well, and that was to watch for the Generals. He was an expert in recognizing them when they were as yet a long way off. He used to slouch against the window panes and keep a keen eye upon the *trottoir* on such days or at such hours as the Generals were likely to appear. Upon catching sight of the oak-leaves in the distance, he would at once notify the ward, so that the orderlies and the nurse could tidy up things before the General made rounds. He had a very keen eye for oak-leaves—the golden oak-leaves on the General's *képi*—and he never by any chance gave a false alarm or mistook a colonel in the distance, and so put us to tidying up unnecessarily. He did not help with the work of course, but continued leaning against the window, reporting the General's progress up the *trottoir*—that he had now gone into Salle III.—that he had left Salle III. and was conversing outside Salle II.—that he was now, positively, on his way up the incline leading into Salle I., and would be upon us any minute. Sometimes the General lingered unnecessarily long on the incline, the wooden slope leading up to the ward, in which case he was not visible from the window, and Erard would amuse us by regretting that he had no periscope for the transom over the door.

There were two Generals who visited the hospital. The big General, the important one, the Commander of the region, who was always beautiful to look upon in his tight, well-fitting black jacket, trimmed with astrakhan, who came from his limousine with a Normandy stick dangling from his wrist, and who wore spotless, clean gloves. This, the big General, came to decorate the men who were entitled to the *Croix de Guerre* and the *Médaille Militaire,* and after he had decorated one or two, as the case might be, he usually continued on through the hospital, shaking hands here and there with the patients, and chatting with the *Directrice* and with the doctors and officers who followed in his wake. The other General was not nearly so imposing. He was short and fat and dressed in a grey-blue uniform, of the shade known as invisible, and his *képi* was hidden by a grey-blue cover, with a little square hole cut out in front, so that an inch of oak-leaves might be seen. He was much more formidable than the big General, however, since he was the *Médecin Inspecteur* of the region, and was responsible for all the hospitals thereabouts. He made rather extensive rounds, closely questioning the surgeons as to the wounds and treatment of each man, and as he was a doctor as well, he knew how to judge of the replies. Whereas the big General was a soldier and not a doctor, and was thus unable to ask any disconcerting questions, so that his visits, while tedious, were never embarrassing. When a General came on the place, it was a signal to down tools. The surgeons would hurriedly finish their operations, or postpone them if possible, and the dressings in the wards were also stopped or postponed, while the surgeons would hurry after the General, whichever one it was, and make deferential rounds with him, if it took all day. And as it usually took at least two hours, the visits of the Generals, one or both, meant considerable interruption to the hospital routine. Sometimes, by chance, both Generals arrived at the same time, which meant that there were double rounds, beginning at opposite ends of the enclosure, and the surgeons were in a quandary as to whose suite they should attach themselves. And the days when it was busiest, when the work was hardest, when there was more than double the staff could accomplish in twenty-four hours, were the days that the Generals usually appeared.

There are some days when it is very bad in a field hospital, just as there are some days when there is nothing to do, and the whole staff is practically idle. The bad days are those when the endless roar of the guns makes the little wooden *baracques* rock and rattle, and when endless processions of ambulances drive in and deliver broken, ruined men, and then drive off again, to return loaded with more wrecks. The beds in the *Salle d'Attente,* where the ambulances unload, are filled with heaps under blankets. Coarse, hobnailed boots stick out from the blankets, and sometimes the heaps, which are men, moan or are silent. On the floor lie piles of clothing, filthy, muddy, blood-soaked, torn or cut from the silent bodies on the beds. The stretcher bearers step over these piles of dirty clothing, or kick them aside, as they lift the shrinking bodies to the brown stretchers, and carry them across one by one, to the operating room. The operating room is filled with stretchers, lying in rows upon the floor, waiting their turn to be emptied, to have their burdens lifted from them to the high operating tables. And as fast as the stretchers are emptied, the stretcher-bearers hurry back to the *Salle d'Attente,* where the ambulances dump their loads, and come over to the operating room again, with fresh lots. Three tables going in the operating room, and the white-gowned surgeons stand so thick around the tables that you cannot see what is on them. There are stretchers lying on the floor of the corridor, and against the walls of the operating room, and more ambulances are driving in all the time.

From the operating room they are brought into the wards, these bandaged heaps from the operating tables, these heaps that once were men. The clean beds of the ward are turned back to receive them, to receive the motionless, bandaged heaps that are lifted, shoved, or rolled from the stretchers to the beds. Again and again, all day long, the procession of stretchers comes into the wards. The foremost bearer kicks open the door with his knee, and lets in ahead of him a blast of winter rain, which sets dancing the charts and papers lying on the table, and blows out the alcohol lamp over which the syringe is boiling. Someone bangs the door shut. The unconscious form is loaded on the bed. He is heavy and the bed sags beneath his weight. The *brancardiers* gather up their red blankets and shuffle off again, leaving cakes of mud and streaks of muddy water on the green linoleum. Outside the guns roar and inside the *baracques* shake, and again and again the stretcher bearers come into the ward, carrying dying men from the high tables in the operating room. They are all that stand between us and the guns, these wrecks upon the beds. Others like them are standing between us and the guns, others like them, who will reach us before morning. Wrecks like these. They are old men, most of them. The old troops, grey and bearded.

There is an attack going on. That does not mean that the Germans are advancing. It just means that the ambulances are busy, for these old troops, these old wrecks upon the beds, are holding up the Germans. Otherwise, we should be swept out of existence. Our hospital, ourselves, would be swept out of existence, were it not for these old wrecks upon the beds. These filthy, bearded, dying men upon the beds, who are holding back the Germans. More like them, in the trenches, are holding back the Germans. By tomorrow these others too, will be with us, bleeding, dying. But there will be others like them in the trenches, to hold back the Germans.

This is the day of an attack. Yesterday was the day of an attack. The day before was the day of an attack. The guns are raising Hell, seven kilometres beyond us, and our *baracques* shakes and tremble with their thunder. These men, grey and bearded, dying in our clean beds, wetting our clean sheets with the blood that oozes from their dressings, have been out there, moaning in the trenches. When they die, we will pull off the bloody sheets, and replace them with fresh, clean ones, and turn them back neatly, waiting for the next agonizing man. We have many beds, and many fresh, clean sheets, and so we are always ready for these old, hairy men, who are standing between us and the Germans.

They seem very weak and frail and thin. How can they do it, these old men? Last summer the young boys did it. Now it is the turn of these old men.

There are three dying in the ward today. It will be better when they die. The German shells have made them ludicrous, repulsive. We see them in this awful interval, between life and death. This interval when they are gross, absurd, fantastic. Life is clean and death is clean, but this interval between the two is gross, absurd, fantastic.

Over there, down at the end, is Rollin. He came in three days ago. A piece of shell penetrated his right eyelid, a little wound so small that it was not worth a dressing. Yet that little piece of *obus* lodged somewhere inside his skull, above his left

The Interval

ear, so the radiographist says, and he's paralyzed. Paralyzed all down the other side, and one supine hand flops about, and one supine leg flops about, in jerks. One bleary eye stays open, and the other eyelid stays shut, over the other bleary eye. Meningitis has set in and it won't be long now, before we'll have another empty bed. Yellow foam blows down his nose, thick yellow foam, bubbles of it, bursting, bubbling yellow foam. It humps up under his nose, up and up, in bubbles, and the bubbles burst and run in turgid streams down upon his shaggy beard. On the wall, above his bed, hang his medals. They are hung up, high up, so he cannot see them. He can't seem them today, because now he is unconscious, but yesterday and the day before, before he got as bad as this, he could see them and it made him cry. He knew he had been decorated *in extremis,* because he was going to die, and he did not want to die. So he sobbed and sobbed all the while the General decorated him, and protested that he did not want to die. He'd saved three men from death, earning those medals, and at the time he never thought of death himself. Yet in the ward he sobbed and sobbed, and protested that he did not want to die.

Back of those red screens is Henri. He is a priest, mobilized as *infirmier.* A good one too, and very tender and gentle with the patients. He comes from the ward next door, Salle II., and is giving extreme unction to the man in that bed, back of the red screens. Peek through the screens and you can see Henri, in his shift sleeves, with a little, crumpled, purple stole around his neck. No, the patient has never regained consciousness since he's been here, but Henri says it's all right. He may be a

{ 35 }

Catholic. Better to take chances. It can't hurt him, anyway, if he isn't. I am glad Henri is back of those red screens. A few minutes ago he came down the ward, in search of absorbent cotton for the Holy Oils, and then he got so interested watching the doctors doing dressings, stayed so long watching them, that I thought he would not get back again, behind the screens, in time.

See that man in the bed next? He's dying too. They trepanned him when he came. He can't speak, but we got his name and regiment from the medal on his wrist. He wants to write. Isn't it funny! He has a block of paper and a pencil, and all day long he writes, writes, on the paper. Always and always, over and over again, he writes on the paper, and he gives the paper to everyone who passes. He's got something on his mind that he wants to get across, before he dies. But no one can understand him. No one can read what he has written—it is just scrawls, scribbles, unintelligible. Day and night, for he never sleeps, he writes on that block of paper, and tears off the sheets and gives them to everyone who passes. And no one can understand, for it is just illegible, unintelligible scribbles. Once we took the paper away to see what he would do and then he wrote with his finger upon the wooden frame of the screen. The same thing, scribbles, but they made no mark on the screen, and he seemed so distressed because they made no mark that we gave him back his paper again, and now he's happy. Or I suppose he's happy. He seems content when we take his paper and pretend to read it. He seems happy, scribbling those words that are words to him but not to us. Careful!

The Interval

Don't stand too close! He spits. Yes, all the time, at the end of every line he spits. Far too. Way across the ward. Don't you see that his bed and the bed next are covered with rubber sheets? That's because he spits. Big spits, too, far across the ward. And always he writes, incessantly, day and night. He writes on that block of paper and spits way across the ward at the end of every line. He's got something on his mind that he wants to get across. Do you think he's thinking of the Germans? He's dying though. He can't spit so far today as he did yesterday.

Death is dignified and life is dignified, but the intervals are awful. They are ludicrous, repulsive.

Is that Erard, calling? Calling that the Generals are coming, both of them, together? Hurry! Tidy up the ward! Rub away the froth from under Rollin's nose! Pull his sheets straight! Take that wet towel, and clean the mackintosh upon that bed and the bed adjoining. See if Henri's finished. Take away the screens. Pull the sheets straight. Tidy up the ward—tell the others not to budge! The Generals are coming!

PARIS
9 May, 1916.

Women and Wives

❧

A BITTER WIND swept in from the North Sea. It swept in over many miles of Flanders plains, driving gusts of rain before it. It was a biting gale by the time it reached the little cluster of wooden huts composing the field hospital, and rain and wind together dashed against the huts, blew under them, blew through them, crashed to pieces a swinging window down at the laundry, and loosened the roof of Salle I. at the other end of the enclosure. It was just ordinary winter weather, such as had lasted for months on end, and which the Belgians spoke of as vile weather, while the French called it vile Belgian weather. The drenching rain soaked into the long, green winter grass, and the sweeping wind was bitter cold, and the howling of the wind was louder than the guns, so that it was only when the wind paused for a moment, between blasts, that the rolling of the guns could be heard.

In Salle I. the stove had gone out. It was a good little stove, but somehow was unequal to struggling with the wind which blew down the long, rocking stove pipe, and blew the fire out. So the little stove grew cold, and the hot water jug on the stove grew cold, and all the patients at that end of the ward likewise grew cold, and demanded hot water bottles, and there wasn't any hot water with which to fill them. So the patients complained and shivered, and in the pauses of the wind, one heard the guns.

Then the roof of the ward lifted about an inch, and more wind beat down, and as it beat down, so the roof lifted. The orderly remarked that if this Belgian weather continued, by tomorrow the roof would be clean off—blown off into the German lines. So all laughed as Fouquet said this, and wondered how they could lie abed with the roof of Salle I., the Salle of the *Grands Blessés,* blown over into the German lines. The ward did not present a neat appearance, for all the beds were pushed about at queer angles, in from the wall, out from the wall, some touching each other, some very far apart, and all to avoid the little leaks of rain which streamed or dropped down from little holes in the roof. This weary, weary war! These long days of boredom in the hospital, these days of incessant wind and rain and cold.

Armand, the chief orderly, ordered Fouquet to rebuild the fire, and Fouquet slipped on his *sabots* and clogged down the ward, away outdoors in the wind, and returned finally with a box of coal on his shoulders, which he dumped heavily on the floor. He was clumsy and sullen, and the coal was wet and mostly slate, and the patients laughed at his efforts to rebuild the fire. Finally, however, it was alight again, and radiated out a faint warmth, which served to bring out the smell of iodoform, and of draining wounds, and other smells which loaded the cold, close air. Then, no one knows who began it, one of the patients showed the nurse a photograph of his wife and child, and in a moment every man in the twenty beds was fishing back of his bed, in his *musette,* under his pillow, for photographs of his wife. They all had wives, it seems, for remember, these were the old troops, who had replaced the young Zouaves who had guarded this part of the Front all summer. One by one they came out, these photographs, from weather-beaten sacks, from shabby boxes, from under pillows, and the nurse must see them all. Pathetic little pictures they were, of common, working-class women, some fat and work-worn, some thin and work-worn, some with stodgy little children grouped about them, some without, but all were practically the same. They were the wives of these men in the beds here, the working-class wives of working-class men—the soldiers of the trenches. Ah yes, France is democratic. It is the Nation's war, and all the men of the Nation, regardless of rank, are serving. But some serve in better places than others. The trenches are mostly reserved for men of the working class, which is reasonable, as there are more of them.

The rain beat down, and the little stove glowed, and the afternoon drew to a close, and the photographs of the wives continued to pass from hand to hand. There was much talk of home, and much of it was longing, and much of it was pathetic, and much of it was resigned. And always the little, ugly wives, the stupid, ordinary wives, represented home. And the words home and wife were interchangeable and stood for the same thing. And the glories and heroisms of war seemed of less interest, as a factor in life, than these stupid little wives.

Then Armand, the chief orderly, showed them all the photograph of his wife. No one knew that he was married, but he said yes, and that he received a letter from her every day— sometimes it was a postcard. Also that he wrote to her every day. We all knew how nervous he used to get, about letter time, when the *vaguemestre* made his rounds, every morning, distributing letters to all the wards. We all knew how impatient he used to get, when the *vaguemestre* laid his letter upon the table, and there it lay, on the table, while he was forced to make rounds with the surgeon, and could not claim it until long afterwards. So it was from his wife, that daily letter, so anxiously, so nervously awaited!

Simon had a wife too. Simon, the young surgeon, German-looking in appearance, six feet of blond brute. But not blond brute really. Whatever his appearance, there was in him something finer, something tenderer, something nobler, to distinguish him from the brute. About three times a week he walked into the ward with his fountain pen between his teeth—he did not smoke, but he chewed his fountain pen—and when the dressings were over, he would tell the nurse, shyly, accidentally, as it were, some little news about his home. Some little incident concerning his wife, some affectionate anecdote about his three young children. Once when one of the staff went over to London on vacation, Simon asked her to buy for his wife a leather coat, such as English women wear, for motoring. Always he thought of his wife, spoke of his wife, planned some thoughtful little surprise or gift for her.

You know, they won't let wives come to the Front. Women can come into the War Zone, on various pretexts, but wives cannot. Wives, it appears, are bad for the morale of the Army. They come with their troubles, to talk of how business is failing, of how things are going to the bad at home, because of the war; of how great the struggle, how bitter the trials and the poverty and hardship. They establish the connecting link between the soldier and his life at home, his life that he is compelled to resign. Letters can be censored and all disturbing items cut out, but if a wife is permitted to come to the War Zone, to see her husband, there is no censoring the things she may tell him. The disquieting, disturbing things. So she herself must be censored, not permitted to come. So for long weary months men must remain at the Front, on active inactivity, and their wives cannot come to see them. Only other people's wives may come. It is not the woman but the wife that is objected to. There is a difference. In war, it is very great.

There are many women at the Front. How do they get there, to the Zone of the Armies? On various pretexts—to see sick relatives, in such and such hospitals, or to see other relatives, brothers, uncles, cousins, other people's husbands—oh, there are many reasons which make it possible for them to come. And always there are the Belgian women, who live in the War Zone, for at present there is a little strip of Belgium left, and all the civilians have not been evacuated from the Army Zone. So there are plenty of women, first and last. Better ones for the officers, naturally, just as the officers' mess is of better quality than that of the common soldiers. But always there are plenty of women. Never wives, who mean responsibility, but just women, who only mean distraction and amusement, just as

{ 43 }

food and wine. So wives are forbidden, because lowering to the morale, but women are winked at, because they cheer and refresh the troops. After the war, it is hoped that all unmarried soldiers will marry, but doubtless they will not marry these women who have served and cheered them in the War Zone. That, again, would be depressing to the country's morale. It is rather paradoxical, but there are those who can explain it perfectly.

No, no, I don't understand. It's because everything has two sides. You would be surprised to pick up a franc, and find Liberty, Equality, and Fraternity on one side, and on the other, the image of the Sower smoothed out. A rose is a fine rose because of the manure you put at its roots. You don't get a medal for sustained nobility. You get it for the impetuous action of the moment, an action quite out of keeping with the trend of one's daily life. You speak of the young aviator who was decorated for destroying a Zeppelin single-handed, and in the next breath you add, and he killed himself, a few days later, by attempting to fly when he was drunk. So it goes. There is a dirty sediment at the bottom of most souls. War, superb as it is, is not necessarily a filtering process, by which men and nations may be purified. Well, there are many people to write you of the noble side, the heroic side, the exalted side of war. I must write you of what I have seen, the other side, the backwash. They are both true. In Spain, they bang their silver coins upon a marble slab, accepting the stamp upon both sides, and then decide whether as a whole they ring true.

Every now and then, Armand, the orderly, goes to the village to get a bath. He comes back with very clean hands and nails, and says that it has greatly solaced him, the warm water. Then later, that same evening, he gets permission to be absent from the hospital, and he goes to our village to a girl. But he is always as eager, as nervous for his wife's letter as ever. It is the same with Simon, the young surgeon. Only Simon keeps himself pretty clean at all times, as he has an orderly to bring him pitchers of hot water every morning, as many as he wants. But Simon has a girl in the village, to whom he goes every week. Only, why does he talk so incessantly about his wife, and show her pictures to me, to everyone about the place? Why should we all be bored with tales of Simon's stupid wife, when that's all she means to him? Only perhaps she means more. I told you I did not understand.

Then the *Gestionnaire,* the little fat man in khaki, who is purveyor to the hospital. Every night he commandeers an ambulance, and drives back into the country, to a village twelve miles away, to sleep with a woman. And the old doctor—he is sixty-four and has grandchildren—he goes down to our village for a little girl of fourteen. He was decorated with the Legion of Honour the other day. It seems incongruous.

Oh yes, of course these were decent girls at the start, at the beginning of the war. But you know women, how they run after men, especially when the men wear uniforms, all gilt buttons and braid. It's not the men's fault that most of the women in the War Zone are ruined. Have you ever watched the village girls when a regiment comes through, or stops for a night or two, *en repos,* on its way to the Front? Have you seen the girls make fools of themselves over the men? Well, that's why there are so many accessible for the troops. Of course the professional prostitutes from Paris aren't admitted to the War Zone, but the Belgian girls made such fools of themselves, the others weren't needed.

Across the lines, back of the German lines, in the invaded districts, it is different. The conquering armies just ruined all the women they could get hold of. Any one will tell you that. *Ces sales Bosches!* For it is inconceivable how any decent girl, even a Belgian, could give herself up voluntarily to a Hun! They used force, those brutes! That is the difference. It's all the difference in the world. No, the women over there didn't make fools of themselves over those men—how could they! No, no. Over there, in the invaded districts, the Germans forced those girls. Here, on this side, the girls cajoled the men till they gave in. Can't you see? You must be pro-German! Any way, they are all ruined and not fit for any decent man to mate with, after the war.

They are pretty dangerous, too, some of these women. No, I don't mean in that way. But they act as spies for the Germans and get a lot of information out of the men, and send it back, somehow, into the German lines. The Germans stop at nothing, nothing is too dastardly, too low, for them to attempt. There were two Belgian girls once, who lived together in a room, in a little village back of our lines. They were natives, and had always lived there, so of course they were not turned out, and when the village was shelled from time to time, they did not seem to mind and altogether they made a lot of money.

Women and Wives

They only received officers. The common soldiers were just dirt to them, and they refused to see them. Certain women get known in a place, as those who receive soldiers and those who receive officers. These girls were intelligent, too, and always asked a lot of intelligent, interested questions, and you know a man when he is excited will answer unsuspectingly any question put to him. The Germans took advantage of that. It is easy to be a spy. Just know what questions you must ask, and it is surprising how much information you can get. The thing is, to know upon what point information is wanted. These girls knew that, it seems, and so they asked a lot of intelligent questions, and as they received only officers, they got a good lot of valuable information, for as I say, when a man is excited he will answer many questions. Besides, who could have suspected at first that these two girls were spies? But they were, as they found out finally, after several months. Their rooms were one day searched, and a mass of incriminating papers were discovered. It seems the Germans had taken these girls from their families—held their families as hostages—and had sent them across into the English lines, with threats of vile reprisals upon their families if they did not produce information of value. Wasn't it beastly! Making these girls prostitutes and spies, upon pain of reprisals upon their families. The Germans knew they were so attractive that they would receive only officers. That they would receive many clients, of high rank, of much information, who would readily fall victims to their wiles. They are very vile themselves, these Germans. The curious thing is, how well they understand how to bait a trap for their enemies.

The Backwash of War

In spite of having nothing in common with them, how well they understand the nature of those who are fighting in the name of Justice, of Liberty and Civilization.

PARIS

4 May, 1916.

Pour la Patrie

⚭

THIS IS HOW IT WAS. It is pretty much always like this in a field hospital. Just ambulances rolling in, and dirty, dying men, and the guns off there in the distance! Very monotonous, and the same, day after day, till one gets so tired and bored. Big things may be going on over there, on the other side of the captive balloons that we can see from a distance, but we are always here, on this side of them, and here, on this side of them, it is always the same. The weariness of it—the sameness of it! The same ambulances, and dirty men, and groans, or silence. The same hot operating rooms, the same beds, always full, in the wards. This is war. But it goes on and on, over and over, day after day, till it seems like life. Life in peace time. It might be life in a big city hospital, so alike is the routine. Only the city hospitals are bigger, and better equipped, and the ambulances are smarter, and the patients don't always come in ambulances—they walk in sometimes, or come in street cars, or in limousines, and they are of both sexes, men and women, and have ever so many things the matter with them—the hospitals of peace time are not nearly so stupid, so monotonous, as the hospitals of war. Bah! War's humane compared to peace! More spectacular, I grant you, more

{ 49 }

acute,—that's what interests us,—but for the sheer agony of life—oh, peace is way ahead!

War is so clean. Peace is so dirty. There are so many foul diseases in peace times. They drag on over so many years, too. No, war's clean! I'd rather see a man die in prime of life, in war time, than see him doddering along in peace time, broken hearted, broken spirited, life broken, and very weary, having suffered many things,—to die at last, at a good, ripe age! How they have suffered, those who drive up to our city hospitals in limousines, in peace time. What's been saved them, those who die young, and clean and swiftly, here behind the guns. In the long run it dots up just the same. Only war's spectacular, that's all.

Well, he came in like the rest, only older than most of them. A shock of iron-grey hair, a mane of it, above heavy, black brows, and the brows were contracted in pain. Shot, as usual, in the abdomen. He spent three hours on the table after admission—the operating table—and when he came over to the ward, they said, not a dog's chance for him. No more had he. When he came out of ether, he said he didn't want to die. He said he wanted to live. Very much. He said he wanted to see his wife again and his children. Over and over he insisted on this, insisted on getting well. He caught hold of the doctor's hand and said he must get well, that the doctor must get him well. Then the doctor drew away his slim fingers from the rough, imploring grasp, and told him to be good and patient.

"Be good! Be patient!" said the doctor, and that was all he could say, for he was honest. What else could he say, knowing that there were eighteen little holes, cut by the bullet, leaking poison into that gashed, distended abdomen? When these little holes, that the doctor could not stop, had leaked enough poison into his system, he would die. Not today, no, but day after tomorrow. Three days more.

So all that first day, the man talked of getting well. He was insistent on that. He was confident. Next day, the second of the three days the doctor gave him, very much pain laid hold of him. His black brows bent with pain and he grew puzzled. How could one live with such pain as that?

That afternoon, about five o'clock, came the General. The one who decorates the men. He had no sword, just a riding whip, so he tossed the whip on the bed, for you can't do an accolade with anything but a sword. Just the *Médaille Militaire*. Not the other one. But the *Médaille Militaire* carries a pension of a hundred francs a year, so that's something. So the General said, very briefly: "In the name of the Republic of France, I confer upon you the *Médaille Militaire*." Then he bent over and kissed the man on his forehead, pinned the medal to the bedspread, and departed.

There you are! Just a brief little ceremony, and perfunctory. We all got that impression. The General has decorated so many dying men. And this one seemed so nearly dead. He seemed half-conscious. Yet the General might have put a little more feeling into it, not made it quite so perfunctory. Yet he's done this thing so many, many times before. It's all right, he does it differently when there are people about, but this time there was no one present—just the doctor, the dying man, and me.

And so we four knew what it meant—just a widow's pension. Therefore there wasn't any reason for the accolade, for the sonorous, ringing phrases of a dress parade—

We all knew what it meant. So did the man. When he got the medal, he knew too. He knew there wasn't any hope. I held the medal before him, after the General had gone, in its red plush case. It looked cheap, somehow. The exchange didn't seem even. He pushed it aside with a contemptuous hand sweep, a disgusted shrug.

"I've seen these things before!" he exclaimed. We all had seen them too. We all knew about them, he and the doctor, and the General and I. He knew and understood, most of all. And his tone was bitter.

After that, he knew the doctor couldn't save him, and that he should not see his wife and children again. Whereupon he became angry with the treatment, and protested against it. The *picqures* hurt—they hurt very much, and he did not want them. Moreover, they did no good, for his pain was now very intense, and he tossed and tossed to get away from it.

So the third day dawned, and he was alive, and dying, and knew that he was dying. Which is unusual and disconcerting. He turned over and over, and black fluid vomited from his mouth into the white enamel basin. From time to time, the orderly emptied the basin, but always there was more, and always he choked and gasped and knit his brows in pain. Once his face broke up as a child's breaks up when it cries. So he cried in pain and loneliness and resentment.

Pour la Patrie

He struggled hard to hold on. He wanted very much to live, but he could not do it. He said: *"Je ne tiens plus."*

Which was true. He couldn't hold on. The pain was too great. He clenched his hands and writhed, and cried out for mercy. But what mercy had we? We gave him morphia, but it did not help. So he continued to cry to us for mercy, he cried to us and to God. Between us, we let him suffer eight hours more like that, us and God.

Then I called the priest. We have three priests on the ward, as orderlies, and I got one of them to give him the Sacrament. I thought it would quiet him. We could not help him with drugs, and he had not got it quite in his head that he must die, and when he said, "I am dying," he expected to be contradicted. So I asked Capolarde to give him the Sacrament, and he said yes, and put a red screen around the bed, to screen him from the ward. Then Capolarde turned to me and asked me to leave. It was summer time. The window at the head of the bed was open, the hay outside was new cut and piled into little haycocks. Over in the distance the guns rolled. As I turned to go, I saw Capolarde holding a tray of Holy Oils in one hand, while with the other he emptied the basin containing black vomitus out the window.

No, it did not bring him comfort, or resignation. He fought against it. He wanted to live, and he resented Death, very bitterly. Down at my end of the ward—it was a silent, summer afternoon—I heard them very clearly. I heard the low words from behind the screen.

The Backwash of War

"Dites: 'Dieu je vous donne ma vie librement pour ma patrie"
(God, I give you my life freely for my country). The priests usually say that to them, for death has more dignity that way. It is
not in the ritual, but it makes a soldier's death more noble. So I
suppose Capolarde said it. I could only judge by the response. I
could hear the heavy, laboured breath, the choking, wailing cry.

"Oui! Oui!" gasped out at intervals. *"Ah mon Dieu! Oui!"*

Again the mumbling, guiding whisper.

"Oui—oui!" came sobbing, gasping, in response.

So I heard the whispers, the priest's whispers, and the stertorous choke, the feeble, wailing, rebellious wailing in response. He was being forced into it. Forced into acceptance.
Beaten into submission, beaten into resignation.

"Oui, oui" came the protesting moans. *"Ah, oui!"*

It must be dawning upon him now. Capolarde is making him
see.

"Oui! Oui!" The choking sobs reach me. *"Ah, mon Dieu,
oui!"* Then very deep, panting, crying breaths:

*"Dieu—je—vous—donne—ma—vie—librement—pour—ma
—patrie!"*

"Librement! Librement! Ah, oui! Oui!" He was beaten at last.
The choking, dying, bewildered man had said the noble words.

"God, I give you my life freely for my country!"

After which came a volley of low toned Latin phrases, rattling in the stillness like the popping of a *mitrailleuse.*

TWO HOURS LATER he was still alive, restless, but no longer
resentful. "It is difficult to go," he murmured, and then: "To-

night, I shall sleep well." A long pause followed, and he opened his eyes.

"Without doubt, the next world is more *chic* than this," he remarked smiling, and then:

"I was mobilized against my inclination. Now I have won the *Médaille Militaire.* My Captain won it for me. He made me brave. He had a revolver in his hand."

A Surgical Triumph

In THE Latin Quarter, somewhere about the intersection of
the Boulevard Montparnasse with the rue de Rennes—it
might have been even a little way back of the Gare
Montparnasse, or perhaps in the other direction where the rue
Vavin cuts into the rue Notre-Dame-des-Champs—any one
who knows the Quarter will know about it at once—there lived
a little hairdresser by the name of Antoine. Some ten years ago
Antoine had moved over from Montmartre, for he was a good
hairdresser and a thrifty soul, and he wanted to get on in life,
and at that time nothing seemed to him so profitable an invest-
ment as to set up a shop in the neighborhood patronized by
Americans. American students were always wanting their hair
washed, so he was told—once a week at least—and in that they
differed from the Russian and Polish and Roumanian and
other students of Paris, a fact which determined Antoine to go
into business at the Montparnasse end of the Quarter, rather
than at the lower end, say round the Pantheon and Saint-
Etienne-du-Mont. And as he determined to put his prices low,
in order to catch the trade, so later on when his business
thrived enormously, he continued to keep them low, in order to
maintain his clients. For if you once get used to having your

{ 57 }

hair washed for two francs, and very well done at that, it is annoying to find that the price has gone up over night to the prices one pays on the Boulevard Capucines. Therefore for ten years Antoine continued to wash hair at two francs a head, and at the same time he earned quite a reputation for himself as a marvellous good person when it came to waves and curls. So that when the war broke out, and his American clients broke and ran, he had a neat, tidy sum saved up, and could be fairly complacent about it all. Moreover, he was a lame man, one leg being some three inches shorter than the other, due to an accident in childhood, so he had never done his military service in his youth, and while not over military age, even yet, there was no likelihood of his ever being called upon to do it. So he stood in the doorway of his deserted shop, for all his young assistants, his curlers and shampooers, had been mobilized, and looked up and down the deserted street, and congratulated himself that he was not in as bad a plight, financially and otherwise, as some of his neighbours.

Next door to him was a restaurant where the students ate, many of them. It had enjoyed a high reputation for cheapness, up to the war, and twice a day had been thronged with a mixed crowd of sculptors and painters and writers, and just dilettantes, which latter liked to patronize it for what they were pleased to call "local colour." Well, look at it now, thought the thrifty Antoine. Everyone gone, except a dozen stranded students who had not money enough to escape, and who, in the kindness of their hearts, continued to eat here "on credit," in order to keep the proprietor going. Even such a fool as the pro-

A Surgical Triumph

prietor must see, sooner or later, that patronage of this sort could lead nowhere, from the point of view of profits—in fact, it was ridiculous.

Antoine, lounging in his doorway, thought of his son. His only son, who, thank God, was too young to enter the army. By the time he was old enough for his military service, the war would all be over—it could not last, at the outside, more than six weeks or a couple of months—so Antoine had no cause for anxiety on that account. The lad was a fine, husky youth, with a sprouting moustache, which made him look older than his seventeen years. He was being taught the art of washing hair, and of curling and dyeing the same, on the human head or aside from it, as the case might be, and he could snap curling irons with a click to inspire confidence in the minds of the most fastidious, so altogether, thought Antoine, he had a good future before him. So the war had no terrors for Antoine, and he was able to speculate freely upon the future of his son, which seemed like a very bright, admirable future indeed, in spite of the disturbances of the moment. Nor did he need to close the doors of his establishment either, in spite of the loss of his assistants, and the loss of his many customers who kept those assistants as well as himself busy. For there still remained in Paris a good many American heads to be washed, from time to time—rather foolhardy, adventurous heads, curious, sensation hunting heads, who had remained in Paris to see the war, or as much of it as they could, in order to enrich their own personal experience. With which point of view Antoine had no quarrel, although there were certain of his

{ 59 }

countrymen who wished these inquisitive foreigners would return to their native land, for a variety of reasons.

As the months rolled along, however, he who had been so farseeing, so thrifty a business man, seemed to have made a mistake. His calculations as to the duration of the war all went wrong. It seemed to be lasting an unconscionable time, and every day it seemed to present new phases for which no immediate settlement offered itself. Thus a year dragged away, and Antoine's son turned eighteen, and his moustache grew to be so imposing that his father commanded him to shave it. At the end of another two months, Antoine found it best to return his son to short trousers, for although the boy was stout and fat, he was not tall, and in short trousers he looked merely an overgrown fat boy, and Antoine was growing rather worried as he saw the lads of the young classes called to the colours. Somewhere, in one of the *Mairies* of Paris—over at Montmartre, perhaps, where he had come from, or at the *Préfecture de Police,* or the *Cité*—Antoine knew that there was a record of his son's age and attainments, which might be used against him at any moment, and as the weeks grew into months, it seemed certain that the class to which this precious son belonged would be called on for military service. Then very hideous weeks followed for Antoine, weeks of nervous suspense and dread. Day by day, as the lad grew in proficiency and aptitude, as he became more and more expert in the matters of his trade, as he learned a delicate, sure touch with the most refractory hair, and could expend the minimum of gas on the drying machine, and the minimum of slap lather, and withal attain the

A Surgical Triumph

best results in pleasing his customers, so grew the danger of
his being snatched away from this wide life spread out before
him, of being forced to fight for his glorious country. Poor fat
boy! On Sundays he used to parade the Raspail with a German
shepherd dog at his heels—bought two years ago as a German
shepherd, but now called a Belgian Police dog—how could he
lay aside his little trousers and become a soldier of France! Yet
every day that time drew nearer, till finally one day the sum-
mons came, and the lad departed, and Antoine closed his shut-
ters for a whole week, mourning desperately. And he was furious against England, which had not made her maximum effort,
had not mobilized her men, had continued with business as
usual, had made no attempt to end the war—wouldn't do so,
until France had become exhausted. And he was furious
against Russia, swamped in a bog of political intrigue, which
lacked organization and munitions and leadership, and was to-
tally unable to drawing off the Bosches on the other frontier,
and delivering a blow to smash them. In fact, Antoine was far
more furious against the Allies of France than against Germany itself. And his rage and grief absolutely overbalanced his
pride in his son, or his ambitions as to his son's possible
achievements. The boy himself did not mind going, when he
was called, for he was something of a fatalist, being so young,
and besides, he could not foresee things. But Antoine, little
lame man, had much imagination and foresaw a great deal.

Mercifully, he could not foresee what actually happened.
Thus it was a shock to him. He learned that his son was
wounded, and then followed many long weeks while the boy

lay in hospital, during which time many kind-hearted Red Cross ladies wrote to Antoine, telling him to be of brave heart and of good courage. And Antoine, being a rich man, in a small hairdressing way, took quite large sums of money out of the bank from time to time, and sent them to the Red Cross ladies, to buy for his son whatever might be necessary to his recovery. He heard from the hospital in the interior—for they were taking most of the wounded to the interior, at that time, for fear of upsetting Paris by the sight of them in the streets—that artificial legs were costly. Thus he steeled himself to the fact that his son would be more hideously lame than he himself. There was some further consultation about artificial arms, rather vague, but Antoine was troubled. Then he learned that a marvellous operation had been performed upon the boy, known as plastic surgery, that is to say, the rebuilding, out of other parts of the body, of certain features of the face that are missing. All this while he heard nothing directly from the lad himself, and in every letter from the Red Cross ladies, dictated to them, the boy begged that neither his father nor his mother would make any attempt to visit him at the hospital, in the interior, till he was ready.

Finally, the lad was "ready." He had been four or five months in hospital, and the best surgeons of the country had done for him the best they knew. They had not only saved his life, but, thanks to his father's money, he had been fitted out with certain artificial aids to the human body which would go far towards making life supportable. In fact, they expressed themselves as extremely gratified with what they had been able to do for the poor young man, nay, they were even proud of him. He was a surgical triumph, and as such they were returning him to Paris, by such and such a train, upon such and such a day. Antoine went to meet the train.

In a little room back of the hairdressing shop, Antoine looked down upon the surgical triumph. This triumph was his son. The two were pretty well mixed up. A passion of love and a passion of furious resentment filled the breast of the little hairdresser. Two very expensive, very good artificial legs lay on the sofa beside the boy. They were nicely jointed and had cost several hundred francs. From the same firm it would also be possible to obtain two very nice artificial arms, light, easily adjustable, well hinged. A hideous flabby heap, called a nose, fashioned by unique skill out of the flesh of his breast, replaced the little snub nose that Antoine remembered. The mouth they had done little with. All the front teeth were gone, but these could doubtless be replaced, in time, by others. Across the lad's forehead was a black silk bandage, which could be removed later, and in his pocket there was an address from which artificial eyes might be purchased. They would have fitted him out with eyes, in the provinces, except that such were better obtainable in Paris. Antoine looked down upon this wreck of his son that lay down before him, and the wreck, not appreciating that he was a surgical triumph, kept sobbing, kept weeping out of his sightless eyes, kept jerking his four stumps in supplication, kept begging in agony:

"Kill me, Papa!"

However, Antoine couldn't do this, for he was civilized.

At the Telephone

❧

AS HE HADN'T DIED in the ambulance, coming from the *Poste de Secours,* the surgeons concluded that they would give him another chance, and risk it on the operating table. He was nearly dead, anyway, so it didn't much matter, although the chance they proposed to give him wasn't even a fighting chance—it was just one in a thousand, some of them put it at one in ten thousand. Accordingly, they cut his clothes off in the *Salle d'Attente,* and carried him, very dirty and naked, to the operating room. Here they found that his ten-thousandth chance would be diminished if they gave him a general anæsthetic, so they dispensed with chloroform and gave him spinal anæsthesia, by injecting something into his spinal canal, between two of the low vertebræ. This completely relieved him of pain, but made him talkative, and when they saw he was conscious like that, it was decided to hold a sheet across the middle of him, so that he could not see what was going on, on the other side of the sheet, below his waist.

The temperature in the operating room was stifling hot, and the sweat poured in drops from the brows of the surgeons, so that it took an orderly, with a piece of gauze, to swab them constantly. However, for all the heat, the man was stone cold and ashen grey, and his nostrils were pinched and dilated, while his breath came in gasps, forty to the minute. Yet, as I say, he was talkative, and his stream of little, vapid remarks, at his end of the sheet, did much to drown the clicking and snapping of clamps on the other side of it, where the surgeons were working to give him his one chance.

A nurse held the sheet on one side of the table, and a priest-orderly held it at the other, and at his head stood a doctor, and the *Directrice* and another nurse, answering the string of vapid remarks and trying to soothe him. And three feet farther along, hidden from him and the little clustering company of people trying to distract his attention, stood the two surgeons, and the two young students, and just the tops of their hair could be seen over the edge of the sheet. They whispered a little from time to time, and worked very rapidly, and there was quite animated talking when the bone saw began to rasp.

The man babbled of his home, and of his wife. He said he wanted to see her again, very much. And the priest-orderly, who wanted to drop his end of the sheet and administer the last Sacrament at once, grew very nervous and uneasy. So the man rambled on, gasping, and they replied to him in soothing manner, and told him that there was a chance that he might see her again. So he talked about her incessantly, and with affection, and his whispered words and the cheery replies quite drowned out the clicking and the snapping of the clamps. After a short while, however, his remarks grew less coherent, and he seemed to find himself back in the trenches, telephoning. He tried hard to telephone, he tried hard to get the connection.

At the Telephone

The wires seemed to be cut, however, and he grew puzzled, and knit his brows and swore, and tried again and again, over and over. He had something to say over the telephone, the trench communication wire, and his mind wandered, and he tried very hard, in his wandering mind, to get the connection. A shell had cut the line evidently. He grew annoyed and restless, and gazed anxiously and perplexedly at the white sheet, held so steadily across his middle. From the waist down he could not move, so all his restlessness took place on the upper side of the sheet, and he was unaware of what was going on on the other side of it, and so failed to hear the incessant rattle of clamps and the subdued whispers from the other side.

He struggled hard to get the connection, in his mind, over the telephone. The wires seemed to be cut, and he cried out in anxiety and distress. Then he grew more and more feeble, and gasped more and more, and became almost inarticulate, in his efforts. He was distressed. But suddenly he got it. He screamed out very loud, relieved, satisfied, triumphant, startling them all.

"*Ça y est, maintenant! Ça y est! C'est le bon Dieu à l'appareil!*"
"(All right now! All right! It is the good God at the telephone!)"

A drop of blood spotted the sheet, a sudden vivid drop which spread rapidly, coming through. The surgeon raised himself.

"Finished here!" he exclaimed with satisfaction.

"Finished here," repeated the *Directrice*.

PARIS
26 June, 1916.

{ 67 }

A Citation

❧

A S A PERSON, Grammont amounted to very little. In private life, before the war broke out, he had been an acrobat in the streets of Paris, and after that he became a hotel boy in some little fifth-rate hotel over behind the Gare St. Lazare. That had proved his undoing, for even the fifth-rate French travelling salesmen and sharpers and adventurers who patronized the hotel had money enough for him to steal. He stole a little, favoured by his position as *garçon d'hôtel*, and the theft had landed him, not in jail, but in the *Bataillon d'Afrique*. He had served in that for two years, doing his military service in the *Bataillon d'Afrique* instead of jail, while working off his five year sentence, and then war being declared, his regiment was transferred from Morocco to France, to Flanders, to the front line trenches, and in course of time he arrived one day at the hospital with a piece of shell in his spleen.

He was pretty ill when brought in, and if he had died promptly, as he should have done, it would have been better. But it happened at that time that there was a surgeon connected with the hospital who was bent on making a reputation for himself, and this consisted in trying to prolong the lives of wounded men who ought normally and naturally to have died. So this surgeon worked hard to save Grammont, and certainly succeeded in prolonging his life, and in prolonging his suffering, over a very considerable portion of time. He worked hard over him, and he used on him everything he could think of, everything that money could buy. Every time he had a new idea as to treatment, no matter how costly it might be, he mentioned it to the *Directrice,* who sent to Paris and got it. All the while Grammont remained in bed, in very great agony, the surgeon making copious notes on the case, noting that under such and such circumstances, under conditions such as the following, such and such remedies and treatment proved futile and valueless. Grammont had a hole in his abdomen, when he entered, about an inch long. After about a month, this hole was scientifically increased to a foot in length, rubber drains stuck out in all directions, and went inwards as well, pretty deep, and his pain was enhanced a hundredfold, while his chances of recovery were not bright. But Grammont had a good constitution, and the surgeon worked hard over him, for if he got well, it would be a wonderful case, and the surgeon's reputation would benefit. Grammont bore it all very patiently, and did not ask to be allowed to die, as many of them did, for since he was of the *Bataillon d'Afrique,* such a request would be equivalent to asking for a remission of sentence—a sentence which the courts averred he justly deserved and merited. They took no account of the fact that his ethics were those of a wandering juggler, turning somersaults on a carpet at the public *fêtes* of Paris, and had been polished off by contact with the men and women he had encountered in his capacity of *garçon d'hôtel*, in a fifth-rate hotel near Montmartre. On the contrary, they rather expected of him the decencies and moralities that come from careful nurture, and these not being forthcoming, they had sent him to the *Bataillon d'Afrique*, where his eccentricities would be of no danger to the public.

So Grammont continued to suffer, over a period of several long months, and he was sufficiently cynical, owing to his short experience of life, to realize that the surgeon, who worked over him so constantly and solicitously, was not solely and entirely disinterested in his efforts to make him well. Grammont had no life to return to, that was the trouble. Everyone knew it. The surgeon knew it, and the orderlies knew it, and his comrades in the adjoining beds knew it—he had absolutely no future before him, and there was not much sense in trying to make him well enough to return to Paris, a hopeless cripple. He lay in hospital for several months, suffering greatly, but greatly patient. During that time, he received no letters, for there was no one to write to him. He was an *apache*, he belonged to a criminal regiment, and he had no family anyhow, and his few friends, tattooed all over the body like himself, were also members of the same regiment, and as such, unable to do much for him in civil life after the war. Such it is to be a *joyeux*, to belong to a regiment of criminals, and to have no family to speak of.

Grammont knew that it would be better for him to die, but he did not like to protest against this painful prolonging of his life. He was pretty well sick of life, but he had to submit to the kind treatment meted out to him, to twist his mouth into a wry smile when the *Directrice* asked him each day if he was not better, and to accept without wincing all the newest devices that the surgeon discovered for him. There was some sense in saving other people's lives, but there was no sense in saving his. But the surgeon, who was working for a reputation, worked hand in hand with the *Directrice* who wanted her hospital to make a reputation for saving the lives of the *grands blessés*. Grammont was the victim of circumstances, as usual, but it was all in his understanding of life, this being caught up in the ambitions of others, so he had to submit.

After about three months of torture, during which time he grew weaker and smelled worse every day, it finally dawned on the nurse that perhaps this life-saving business was not wholly desirable. If he got "well," in the mildest acceptation of the term, he would be pretty well disabled, and useless and good for nothing. And if he was never going to get well, for which the prospects seemed bright enough, why force him along through more weeks of suffering, just to try out new remedies? Society did not want him, and he had no place in it. Besides, he had done his share, in the trenches, in protecting its best traditions.

Then they all began to notice, suddenly, that in bed Grammont was displaying rather nice qualities, such as you would not expect from a *joyeux,* a social outcast. He appeared to be extremely patient, and while his face twisted up into knots of pain, most of the time, he did not cry out and disturb the ward as he might have done. This was nice and considerate, and other good traits were discovered too. He was not a nuisance, he was not exacting, he did not demand unreasonable things, or refuse to submit to unreasonable things, when these were demanded of him. In fact, he seemed to accept his pain as God-given, and with a fatalism which in some ways was rather admirable. He could not help smelling like that, for he was full of rubber drains and of gauze drains, and if the doctor was too busy to dress his wounds that day, and so put him off till the next, it was not his fault for smelling so vilely. He did not raise any disturbance, nor make any complaint, on certain days when he seemed to be neglected. Any extra discomfort that he was obliged to bear, he bore stoically. Altogether, after some four months of this, it was discovered that Grammont had rather a remarkable character, a character which merited some sort of recognition. He seemed to have rather heroic qualities of endurance, of bravery, of discipline. Nor were they the heroic qualities that suddenly develop in a moment of exaltation, but on the contrary, they were developed by months of extreme agony, of extreme bodily pain. He could have been so disagreeable, had he chosen. And as he cared so little to have his life saved, his goodness could not have been due to that. It seemed that he was merely very decent, very considerate of others, and wanted to give as little trouble as he could, no matter what took place. Only he got thinner and weaker, and more and more gentle, and at last after five months of this, the *Directrice* was touched by his conduct and suggested that here was a case of heroism as well worthy of the *Croix de Guerre* as were the more spectacular movements on the battlefield. It took a few weeks longer, of gentle suggestion on her part, to convey this impression to the General, but at last the General entered into correspondence with the officers of the regiment to which Grammont belonged, and it then transpired that as a soldier Grammont had displayed the same qualities of consideration for others and of discipline, that he was now displaying in a hospital bed. Finally one day, the news came that Grammont was to be decorated. Everyone else in the ward, who deserved it, had been decorated long ago, naturally, for they had not belonged to the *Bataillon d'Afrique*. Their services had been recognized long ago. Now, however, after these many months of suffering, Grammont was to receive the *Croix de Guerre*. He was nearly dead by this time. When told the news, he smiled faintly. He did not seem to care. It seemed to make very little impression upon him. Yet it should have made an impression, for he was a convicted criminal, and it was a condescension that he should be so honoured at all. He had somehow won this honour, this token of forgiveness, by suffering so long, so uncomplainingly. However, a long delay took place, although finally his papers came, his citation, in which he was cited in the orders of the regiment as having done a very brave deed, under fire. He smiled a little at that. It had taken place so long ago, this time when he had done the deed, received the wound that kept him suffering so long. It seemed so little worth while to acknowledge it now, after all these months, when he was just ready to leave.

Then more delay took place, and Grammont got weaker, and the orderlies said among themselves that if the General was

A Citation

ever going to decorate this man, that he had better hurry up. However, so long a time had passed that it did not much matter. Grammont was pleased with his citation. It seemed to make it all right for him, somehow. It seemed to give him standing among his fellow patients. The hideous tattoo marks on his arms and legs, chest and back, which proclaimed him an *apache,* which showed him such every time his wound was dressed, were about to be overlaid with a decoration for bravery upon the field of battle. But still the General did not come. Grammont grew very weak and feeble and his patience became exhausted. He held on as long as he could. So he died finally, after a long pull, just twenty minutes before the General arrived with his medals.

PARIS
27 June, 1916

{ 75 }

The Forbidden Zone

MARY BORDEN

Preface

❧

I HAVE NOT invented anything in this book. The sketches and poems were written between 1914 and 1918, during four years of hospital work with the French Army. The five stories I have written recently from memory; they recount true episodes that I cannot forget.

I have called the collection of fragments "The Forbidden Zone" because the strip of land immediately behind the zone of fire where I was stationed went by that name in the French Army. We were moved up and down inside it; our hospital unit was shifted from Flanders to the Somme, then to Champagne, and then back again to Belgium, but we never left "La Zone Interdite."

To those who find these impressions confused, I would say that they are fragments of a great confusion. Any attempt to reduce them to order would require artifice on my part and would falsify them. To those on the other hand who find them unbearably plain, I would say that I have blurred the bare horror of facts and softened the reality in spite of myself, not because I wished to do so, but because I was incapable of a nearer approach to the truth.

I have dared to dedicate these pages to the Poilus who

passed through our hands during the war, because I believe they would recognise the dimmed reality reflected in these pictures. But the book is not meant for them. They know, not only everything that is contained in it, but all the rest that can never be written.

THE AUTHOR.

Belgium

❦

MUD: and a thin rain coming down to make more mud. Mud: with scraps of iron lying in it and the straggling fragment of a nation, lolling, hanging about in the mud on the edge of disaster.

It is quiet here. The rain and the mud muffle the voice of the war that is growling beyond the horizon. But if you listen you can hear cataracts of iron pouring down channels in the sodden land, and you feel the earth trembling.

Back there is France, just behind the windmill. To the north, the coast; a coast without a port, futile. On our right? That's the road to Ypres. The less said about that road the better: no one goes down it for choice—it's British now. Ahead of us, then? No, you can't get out that way. No, there's no frontier, just a bleeding edge, trenches. That's where the enemy took his last bite, fastened his iron teeth, and stuffed to bursting, stopped devouring Belgium, left this strip, these useless fields, these crumpled dwellings.

Cities? None. Towns? No whole ones. Yes, there are half a dozen villages. But there is plenty of mud, and a thin silent rain falling to make more mud—mud with things lying in it, wheels, broken motors, parts of houses, graves.

The Forbidden Zone

This is what is left of Belgium. Come, I'll show you. Here are trees drooping along a canal, ploughed fields, roads leading into sand dunes, roofless houses. There's a farm, an old woman with a crooked back feeding chickens, a convoy of motor lorries round a barn; they squat like elephants. And here is a village crouching in the mud: the cobblestone street is slippery and smeared with refuse, and there is a yellow cat sitting in a window. This is the headquarters of the Belgian Army. You see those men, lolling in the doorways—uncouth, dishevelled, dirty? They are soldiers. You can read on their heavy jowls, in their stupefied, patient, hopeless eyes, how boring it is to be a hero.

The king is here. His office is in the schoolroom down the street, a little way past the church, just beyond the dung heap. If we wait we may see him. Let's stand with these people in the rain and wait.

A band is going to play to the army. Yes, I told you, this is the army—these stolid men standing aimlessly in the drizzle, and these who come stumbling along the slippery ditches, and those leaning in degraded doorways. They fought their way out of Liége and Namur, followed the king here; they are what is left of plucky little Belgium's heroic army.

And the song of the nation that comes from the horns in the front of the wine shop, the song that sounds like the bleating of sheep, can it help them? Can it deceive them? Can it whisk from their faces the stale despair, the unutterable boredom, and brighten their disappointed eyes? They are so few, and they have nothing to do but stand in the rain waiting. When the band stops they will disappear into the estaminet to warm their stomachs with wine and cuddle the round-cheeked girls. What else can they do? The French are on one side of them, the British on the other, and the enemy in front. They cannot go back; to go back is to retreat, and they have been retreating ever since they can remember. They can retreat no farther. This village is where they stop. At one end of it is a pigsty, at the other end is a grave-yard, and all about are flats of mud. Can the noise, the rhythmical beating of the drum, the piping, the hoarse shrieking, help these men, make them believe, make them glad to be heroes? They have nowhere to go now and nothing to do. There is nothing but mud all about, and a soft fine rain coming down to make more mud—mud with a broken fragment of a nation lolling in it, hanging about waiting in it behind the shelter of a disaster that has been accomplished.

Come away, for God's sake—come away. Let's go back to Dunkerque. The king? Didn't you see him? He came out of the schoolhouse some time ago and drove away toward the sand-dunes—a big fair man in uniform. You didn't notice? Never mind. Come away.

The Square

❦

ELOW MY WINDOW in the big bright square a struggle
is going on between the machines of war and the people of the town. There are the motor cars of the army,
the limousines, and the touring cars and the motor lorries and
the ambulances; and there are the little bare-headed women of
the town with baskets on their arms who try to push the mon-
sters out of their way.

The motors come in and go out of the four corners of the
square, and they stand panting and snorting in the middle of it.
The limousines are full of smart men in uniforms with silver
hair and gold braid on their round red hats. The touring cars,
too, are full of uniforms, but on the faces of the young men
who drive them is a look of exhaustion and excitement. The
motors make a great noise and a great smell and a great dust.
They come into the square, hooting and shrieking; they draw
up in the square with grinding brakes. The men in them get
out with a flourish of capes: they stamp on the pavement with
heavy boots; they salute one another stiffly like wooden toys,
then disappear into the buildings where they hold murderous
conferences and make elaborate plans of massacre.

The motor cars have all gone wrong. They are queer. They

are not doing what they were designed to do when they were turned out of the factories. The limousines were made to carry ladies to places of amusement: they are carrying generals to places of killing. The limousines and the touring cars and the motor lorries are all debauched; they have a depraved look; their springs sag, their wheels waver; their bodies lean to one side. The elegant limousines that carry the generals are crusted with old mud; the leather cushions of the touring cars are in tatters; the great motor lorries crouch under vast burdens. They crouch in the square ashamed, deformed, very weary; their unspeakable burdens bulge under canvas coverings. Only the snobbish ambulances with the red crosses on their sides have self-assurance. They have the self-assurance of amateurs.

The business of killing and the business of living go on together in the square beneath the many windows, jostling each other.

The little women of the town are busy; they are dressed in black; they have children with them. Some lead children by the hand, others are big with children yet unborn. But all the women are busy. They ignore the motors; they do not see the fine scowling generals, nor the strained excited faces in the fast touring cars, nor the provisions of war under their lumpy coverings. They do not even wonder what is in the ambulances. They are too busy. They scurry across to the shops, instinctively dodging, and come out again with bundles; they talk to each other a little without smiling; they stare in front of them; they are staring at life; they are thinking about the business of living.

The Square

On Saturdays they put up their booths on the cobblestones and hold their market. The motors have to go round another way on market days. There is no room in the square for the generals, nor for the dying men in the ambulances. The women are there. They buy and sell their saucepans and their linen and their spools of thread and their fowls and their flowers; they bargain and they chatter; they provide for their houses and their children; they give oranges to their children, and put away their coppers in their deep pockets.

As for the men on the stretchers inside the smart ambulances with the bright red crosses, they do not know about the women in the square. They cannot hear their chattering, nor see the children sucking oranges; they can see nothing and hear nothing of the life that is going on in the square; they are lying on their backs in the dark canvas bellies of the ambulances, staring at death. They do not know that on Saturday mornings their road does not lie through the big bright square because the little women of the town are busy with their market.

Moonlight

❧

T HE MOONLIGHT is a pool of silver on the linoleum floor. It glints on the enamel washbasin and slop pail. I can almost see the moon reflected in the slop pail. Everything in my cubicle is luminous. My clothes hanging on pegs, my white aprons and rubber boots, my typewriter and tin box of biscuits, the big sharp scissors on the table—all these familiar things are touched with magic and make me uneasy. Through the open door of the hut comes the sweet sickish scent of new-mown hay, mingling with the smell of disinfectants, of Eau de Javel and iodoform, and wet mud and blood. There is wet mud on my boots and blood on my apron. I don't mind. It is the scent of new-mown hay that makes me uneasy. The little whimpering voice of a man who is going to die in an hour or two comes across the whispering grass from the hut next door. That little sound I understand. It is like the mew of a wounded cat. Soon it will stop. It will stop soon after midnight. I know. I can tell. I go on duty at midnight, and he will die and go to Heaven soon after, lulled to sleep by the lullaby of the guns.

Far beyond him, out in the deep amorous night, I can hear the war going on. I hear the motor convoys rumbling down the road and the tramp of feet marching. I can tell the ambulances from the lorries and distinguish the wagons that carry provisions. Reinforcements are coming up along the road through the moonlit fields. The three-inch guns are pounding. All along the horizon they are pounding, pounding. But there will be no attack. The section is quiet. I know. I can tell. The cannonade is my lullaby. It soothes me. I am used to it. Every night it lulls me to sleep. If it stopped I could not sleep. I would wake with a start. The thin wooden walls of my cubicle tremble and the windows rattle a little. That, too, is natural. It is the whispering of the grass and the scent of new-mown hay that makes me nervous.

The war is the world, and this cardboard house, eight by nine, behind the trenches, with a roof that leaks and windows that rattle, and an iron stove in the corner, is my home in it. I have lived here ever since I can remember. It had no beginning, it will have no end. War, the Alpha and the Omega, world without end—I don't mind it. I am used to it. I fit into it. It provides me with everything that I need, an occupation, a shelter, companions, a jug and a basin. When winter comes my stove is red hot, and I sit with my feet on it. When it rains I sleep under a mackintosh sheet with an umbrella over my pillow and a basin on my feet. Sometimes in a storm the roof blows off. Then I wait under the blankets for the old men to come and put it back again. Sometimes the Germans shell the cross roads beyond us or the town behind us, and the big shells pass over the hospital screaming. Then the surgeons in the operating hut turn up the collars of their white jackets, and we lift our shoulders round our ears. I don't mind—it is part of the routine. For companions there are, of course, the surgeons and the nurses and the old grizzled orderlies, but I have other companions more intimate than these. Three in particular, a lascivious monster, a sick bad-tempered animal, and an angel; Pain, Life and Death. The first two are quarrelsome. They fight over the wounded like dogs over a bone. They snarl and growl and worry the pieces of men that we have here; but Pain is the stronger. She is the greater. She is insatiable, greedy, vilely amorous, lustful, obscene—she lusts for the broken bodies we have here. Wherever I go I find her possessing the men in their beds, lying in bed with them; and Life, the sick animal, mews and whimpers, snarls and barks at her, till Death comes—the Angel, the peace-maker, the healer, whom we wait for, pray for—comes silently, drives Pain away, and horrid, snarling Life, and leaves the man in peace.

Lying in my bed, I listen to the great, familiar, muttering voice of the war and to the feeble, mewing, whimpering voice of Life, the sick bad-tempered animal, and to the loud triumphant guttural shouts of Pain plying her traffic in the hut next to me, where the broken bodies of men are laid out in rows with patches of moonlight on their coverlets. At midnight I will get up and put on a clean apron and go across the grass to the sterilizing room and get a cup of cocoa. At midnight we always have cocoa in there next to the operating room, because there is a big table and boiling water. We push back the drums of clean dressings and the litter of soiled bandages, and drink our cocoa standing round the table. Sometimes there isn't much room. Sometimes legs and arms wrapped in cloths have to be pushed out of the way. We throw them on the floor—they belong to no one and are of no interest to anyone—and drink our cocoa. The cocoa tastes very good. It is part of the routine.

But the moonlight is like a pool of silver water on the floor, and the air is soft and the moon is floating, floating through the sky. In a dream I see her, in a crazy hurting dream. Lovely night, lovely lunatic moon, lovely scented love-sick earth—you are not true; you are not a part of the routine. You are a dream, an intolerable nightmare, and you recall a world that I once knew in a dream.

The mewing voice of the wounded cat dying in the shed next door to me is true. He is my brother, that wounded cat. This also is true. His voice goes on and on. He tells the truth to me. He tells me what I know to be true. But soon—quite soon—I hope and think that his voice will stop. Now the monstrous mistress that he has taken to his bed has got him, but soon he will escape. He will go to sleep in her arms lulled by the lullaby of the pounding guns that he and I are used to, and then in his sleep the Angel will come and his soul will slip away. It will run lightly over the whispering grasses and murmuring trees. It will leap through the velvety dark that is tufted with the soft concussion of distant shells bursting from the mouths of cannon. It will fly up through the showery flares and shooting rockets past the moon into Heaven. I know this is true. I know it must be true.

How strange the moon is with its smooth cheeks. How I fear the whispering of the grasses and murmuring of the trees.

Moonlight

What are they saying? I want to go to sleep to the old soothing lullaby of the cannon that rocks me—rocks me in my cradle—but they keep me awake with their awful whispering. I am drowsy and drugged with heavy narcotics, with ether and iodoform and other strong odours. I could sleep. I could sleep with the familiar damp smell of blood on my apron, but the terrible scent of the new-mown hay disturbs me. Crazy peasants came and cut it while the battle was going on just beyond the canal. Women and children came with pitch-forks and tossed it in the sun. Now it lies over the road in the moonlight, wafting its distressing perfume into my window, bringing me waking dreams—unbearable, sickening, intolerable dreams—that interrupt the routine.

Ah! The great gun down by the river is roaring, is shouting. What a relief! That I understand—that giant's voice. He is a friend—another familiar, monstrous friend. I know him. I listen every night for his roar. I long to hear it. But it is dying away now. The echo goes growling down the valley, and again the trees and the grasses begin that murmuring and whispering. They are lying. It is a lie that they are saying. There are no lovely forgotten things. The other world was a dream. Beyond the gauze curtains of the tender night there is War, and nothing else but War. Hounds of war, growling, howling; bulls of war, bellowing, snorting; war eagles, shrieking and screaming; war fiends banging at the gates of Heaven, howling at the open gates of hell. There is War on the earth—nothing but War, War let loose in the world, War—nothing left in the whole world but War—War, world without end, amen.

The Forbidden Zone

I must change my apron now and go out into the moonlight. The sick man is still mewing. I must go to him. I am afraid to go to him. I cannot bear to go across the whispering grass and find him in the arms of his monstrous paramour. It is a night made for love, for love, for love. That is not true. That is a lie.

The peaked roofs of the huts stand out against the lovely sky. The moon is just above the abdominal ward. Next to it is the hut given up to gas gangrene, and next to that are the Heads. The Knees are on the other side, and the Elbows and the fractured Thighs. A nurse comes along carrying a lantern. Her white figure moves silently across the ground. Her lantern glows red in the moonlight. She goes into the gangrene hut that smells of swamp gas. She won't mind. She is used to it, just as I am. Pain is lying in there waiting for her. It is holding the damp greenish bodies of the gangrene cases in her arms. The nurse will try to get her out of those beds, but the loathsome creature will be too much for her. What can the nurse do against this she-devil, this Elemental, this Diva? She can straighten a pillow, pour drops out of a bottle, pierce a shrunken side with a needle. She can hold to lips a cup of cold water. Will that land her, too, in Heaven one day? I wonder; I doubt it. She is no longer a woman. She is dead already, just as I am—really dead, past resurrection. Her heart is dead. She killed it. She couldn't bear to feel it jumping in her side when Life, the sick animal, choked and rattled in her arms. Her ears are deaf; she deafened them. She could not bear to hear Life crying and mewing. She is blind so that she cannot see the torn parts of men she must handle. Blind, deaf, dead—she is

Moonlight

strong, efficient, fit to consort with gods and demons—a machine inhabited by the ghost of a woman—soulless, past redeeming, just as I am—just as I will be.

There are no men here, so why should I be a woman? There are heads and knees and mangled testicles. There are chests with holes as big as your fist, and pulpy thighs, shapeless; and stumps where legs once were fastened. There are eyes—eyes of sick dogs, sick cats, blind eyes, eyes of delirium; and mouths that cannot articulate; and parts of faces—the nose gone, or the jaw. There are these things, but no men; so how could I be a woman here and not die of it? Sometimes, suddenly, all in an instant, a man looks up at me from the shambles, a man's eyes signal or a voice calls "Sister! Sister!" Sometimes suddenly a smile flickers on a pillow, white, blinding, burning, and I die of it. I feel myself dying again. It is impossible to be a woman here. One must be dead.

Certainly they were men once. But now they are no longer men.

There has been a harvest. Crops of men were cut down in the fields of France where they were growing. They were mown down with a scythe, were gathered into bundles, tossed about with pitchforks, pitchforked into wagons and transported great distances and flung into ditches and scattered by storms and gathered up again and at last brought here—what was left of them.

Once they were real, splendid, ordinary, normal men. Now they mew like kittens. Once they were fathers and husbands and sons and the lovers of women. Now they scarcely remember. Sometimes they call to me "Sister, Sister!" in the faint voices of far-away men, but when I go near them and bend over them, I am a ghost woman leaning over a thing that is mewing; and it turns away its face and flings itself back into the arms of Pain, its monster bedfellow. Each one lies in the arms of this creature. Pain is the mistress of each one of them.

Not one can escape her. Neither the very old ones nor the young slender ones. Their weariness does not protect them, nor their loathing, nor their struggling, nor their cursing. Their hideous wounds are no protection, nor the blood that leaks from their wounds on to the bedclothes, nor the foul odour of their festering flesh. Pain is attracted by these things. She is a harlot in the pay of War, and she amuses herself with the wreckage of men. She consorts with decay, is addicted to blood, cohabits with mutilations, and her delight is the refuse of suffering bodies.

You can watch her plying her trade here any day. She is shameless. She lies in their beds all day. She lies with the Heads and the Knees and the festering Abdomens. She never leaves them. Even when she has exhausted them, even when at last worn out with her frenzy they drop into a doze, she lies beside them, to tease them with her excruciating caresses, her pinches and twinges that make them moan and twist in sleep. At any hour of the day or night you can watch her deadly amours, and watch her victims struggling, The wards are full of these writhings and tossings, they are agitated as if by a storm with her obscene antics. But if you come at midnight—if you come with me now—you will see the wounded, helpless, go

Moonlight

fast asleep in her arms. You will see them abandon themselves to deep sleep with her beside them in their beds. They hope to escape her in sleep and find their way back to the fields where they were growing, strong lusty men, before they were cut down.

She lies there to spoil their dreams. When they dream of their women and little children, of their mothers and sweethearts; when they dream that they are again clean, normal, real men, filled with a tender and lovely love for women, then she wakes them. In the dark she wakes them and tightens her arms round their shrivelled bodies. She strangles their cries. She pours her poisoned breath into their panting mouths. She squeezes their throbbing hearts in their sides. In the dark, in the dark she takes them; she takes them to herself and keeps them until Death comes, the gentle angel. This is true. I know. I have seen.

Listen. Do you hear him? He is still mewing like a cat, but very faintly, and the trees are still murmuring and the grasses whispering. I hear the sound of many large creatures moving behind the hedge. They are panting and snorting. A procession of motor lorries and ambulances is going heavily down the road. They pass slowly, lumbering along with their heavy loads, and through the huge laborious sound of their grinding wheels threads the whirr of a swift touring car. You can hear it coming in the distance. It rushes nearer. It dashes past with a scratching shriek of its Klaxon. It plunges down the road and is gone. Some officer hurrying on some terrible business, some officer with gold leaves on his hat and a sword on his hip, in a limousine, leaning back on his cushions, calculating the number of men needed to repair yesterday's damage, and the number of sandbags required to repair their ditches. He does not see the lovely night and the lovely moon, and the unseemly love affair that is going on between the earth and the moon. He does not notice that he has passed the gate of a hospital, or know that behind the hedge men are lying in the dark with patches of blood and patches of moonlight on their coverlets. He is blind, deaf, dead, as I am—another machine just as I am.

It is twelve o'clock. The nurse has disappeared. She has left her lantern outside my door. There is no one to be seen. Nothing moves in the moonlight. But the earth is trembling, and the throbbing of the guns is the throbbing of the pulse of the War; world without end.

Listen! The whimpering mew of the wounded cat has stopped. There's not a sound except the whisper of the wind in the grass. Quick! Be quick! In a moment a man's spirit will escape, will be flying through the night past the pale, beautiful, sentimental face of the moon.

Enfant de Malheur

❧

IS NAME was tattooed on his arm, and the head of a woman life-size on his back. He himself might have been fashioned by Praxiteles, but some sailor in a North African port had dug needles of blue ink into the marble flesh of his arm, and written there the indelible words—Enfant de Malheur. He waved that slender member of his incredibly perfect Greek body in the nurse's face when she asked him his name, and said Voilà! with a biting sarcasm and a snarl of pointed white teeth. Then, glaring defiance, defying her to knife him in the back, he turned over and displayed his back to her. The face of a chocolate box beauty done in colours decorated its smooth surface. Her silly blue eyes stared up from between his fine flat shoulder blades and her full red lips smiled on his spinal cord. She was a trashy creature, a plump, coarse morsel, no fit companion for this young prince of darkness. He had race, distinction, an exquisite elegance, and, even in his battered state, the savage grace of a panther. Not even his wounds could disfigure him. The long deep gash in his side made his smooth torso seem the more incredibly fair and frail. The loss of one leg rendered the other more exquisite with its round polished knee and slim ankle.

The Forbidden Zone

He was one of a lot of some twenty apaches that had been brought in that morning. As I remember them, they were all handsome young men—these assassins, thieves, pimps and traffickers in drugs—with sleek elastic limbs, smooth polished skins and beautiful bones. It was, if I remember rightly, only about their heads that I noticed imperfection. Their skulls were not quite right somehow, nor the shape of their ears. Their foreheads were low and receding, their jaws weak, and their mouths betrayed depravity. Still they were beautiful, beautiful as young leopards, and they brought with them into the hospital the strange morbid glamour of crime. But the Enfant de Malheur was the most beautiful of them all. He had the face of an angel.

They were exiles, and they belonged to the Bataillons d'Afrique that had been put into the line two days before on the eve of an attack. Excellent troops of assault, these young Parisian criminals who had been sentenced to penal servitude for life and conscripted in the army of North Africa; but no good for holding the line or for anything else, so the General told me. No stamina, no powers of endurance; but they were born killers and they went over the top when the signal was given like wolf-hounds suddenly unleashed. Moreover, they knew that if they distinguished themselves in battle they would win back their freedom and become again at the end of the war, citizens of Paris.

Paris! Montmartre! The lighted cafés of the Place Blanche; the jingling, flashing, merry boulevards; these boys who lay like Greek gods in their beds recalled fantastically all the romantic

tales that had ever been written by liars about the underworld
of that most brilliant and seductive of capitals. The cunning
camouflage of their beauty made it all seem true. The wild
breath of false romance swept down the huts over their beds.
And they lay in their beds, glaring, defiant, suspicious, expecting, so it seemed, to be attacked, assassinated or robbed in
their beds at any moment by any one of us.

Their arrival had created something of a sensation in the
hospital. The line had been held for the last few weeks by regi-
ments of territorials, the "old ones," as we called them; and we
had received for many days nothing but greybeards. Fathers
and grandfathers. "Vieux Pères," good troops they made for
holding the line in the wet winter weather. They simply sat
there doggedly in the cold, the mud and the wet, enduring the
war and getting rheumatism in their old joints week after week.
So the arrival of this gang of reckless, noisy, sardonic and suspicious cut-throats was a pleasant diversion. But the Médicin
Chef wasn't pleased. He divided them up carefully, put only
two, or at the most three, in each hut, and turned the nurses
out of the operating room, for when these lovely beings were
laid out in their immaculate beauty on the operating table and
the ether mask was put over their proud, depraved, contemptuous faces, a stream of language of such foulness spurted from
their chiselled lips that even the surgeons turned sick.

Pim ignored this. Pim was in charge of the Enfant de
Malheur. She was the daughter of an Archdeacon, and had
been brought up in a cathedral close in the north of England,
then had trained in Edinburgh. She was an excellent nurse,

very fastidious about the care of the patients. Her blue uniform was always stiffly starched, her cap and apron were immaculate; so was her smooth severe Madonna face, with its childlike candid eyes and thin quiet mouth. Pim didn't understand the word "apache." She didn't understand the Enfant de Malheur. She didn't, I believe, notice that he was beautiful. She was interested in his wounds and in saving his life. She had come to the front to nurse the French because she had been told that they needed nurses more in the French Army than in England; but she was not interested in Frenchmen, nor in any man. She knew no men. She knew only her patients. And she fought for their lives grimly, quietly, with her thin gentle lips pressed tight together when the crisis came. So she did not look at her young apache with curiosity, and she did not know why he glared at her or why he gave a start and leapt sideways in his bed when she approached him. She made no attempt at understanding his queer argot, and was unaware when he insulted her. She quite simply continued to look after him with complete serenity. She simply went on handling his dangerous body with the perfectly assured impersonal gentleness of an excellent surgical nurse—washing him, dressing his wounds, giving him injections, enemas and bed pans, as if she were at home in Edinburgh at work under the eye of the most exacting of Scotch surgeons.

It was Guerin who understood that the pain-racked body of the Enfant de Malheur was as dangerous as an unexploded bomb. Guerin was an orderly with the rank of corporal, and he shared with Pim the responsibility of the ward. He was a priest, mobilized for the war; but we forgot this the greater part of the time, because he was so efficient as a nurse and looked so little like a priest in his neat blue corporal's uniform with his bright alert eyes looking out through his pince-nez. Indeed, it was only when one of Pim's patients died that we remembered that Guerin was a priest. Then Pim summoned him shyly and withdrew, leaving Guerin alone with the man who was dying.

Sometimes coming in I would find the little man kneeling by a bedside with a crucifix in his hands, and the sight of his neat compact figure and intent scholarly face would recall to me his other holy calling, and make me wonder. He was so unlike the big priest in the black cassock with the white head bandage, who strode through the hospital grounds swinging a walking stick, and who had won the Croix de Guerre with three palms for bravery in the field. Guerin had looked to me, when he first came to us, a bit of a prig. He had a slightly quizzical expression; his manner was dry and impersonal; but he was on duty at six in the morning, and although he was supposed to go off twelve hours later, he was usually there busy with Pim until late in the evening, swabbing tables, boiling up instruments, or writing letters to someone's dictation.

They were a very satisfactory couple. They scarcely spoke to each other, but they worked together as if they had been born for this, and this alone—this silent, quick, watchful, unceasing battle with death; this struggle to save men's lives, by doing small things accurately at the right moment—without fuss, without noise, without sign of fatigue or hurry, or nervousness or despair. Their hands, their feet, their eyes never faltered and were never still. They made the same calm, quick, exact movements, took no unnecessary steps, left nothing undone. Yes, a curiously harmonious pair, this tall English woman and small sturdy Frenchman. But Guerin did more than Pim did, because he understood more and had more to do. He believed in the Holy Catholic Church and the Remission of Sins and the Life Everlasting. He had set himself a task that he never mentioned. These wounded were not only his countrymen, they were his children, and he considered himself responsible for their immortal souls.

So he frowned and his small sharply-cut features took on a look of added sharpness and his keen eyes grew suddenly alert when the stretcher-bearers brought the Enfant de Malheur into the ward. He didn't interfere with Pim, but he watched. He didn't warn her or try to stop her, or keep her away from the lovely Greek god whom he knew to be one of the damned and a fiend out of hell; but when she leaned over the beautiful fierce chiselled face he was always on the watch. And so he saw what Pim, who didn't understand, couldn't see. He saw that this damné, this vile savage rat from the sewers of Paris, was puzzled, bewildered, intimidated by Pim's stolid impersonal gentleness. He saw him gradually stop jumping to one side of the bed and take to wriggling and squirming with acute discomfort under her candid gaze, and he heard him muttering and snarling under his breath with exasperation at the insufferable presence of this Madonna-like woman with the cold, white, calm face. Guerin understood how uncomfortable the Enfant de Malheur would be in the presence of the beautiful Mother of

Enfant de Malheur

God, and he watched him wriggle to avoid Pim's cool maiden eyes. And so on the third day, when the apache beckoned Pim to come to him, Guerin was even more surprised than Pim was, because he knew that the wicked brute in the boy had been tamed by the power of Pim's unconscious serenity. Pim approached calmly. She was rather a stupid woman in some ways. "What is it?" she asked in her virginal English voice. "Que voulez-vous?" And Guerin, listening, watchful still, but with his tense face relaxed a little, heard the apache whisper as he pulled Pim down: "Come close. I want to tell you something. I want to tell you," said the child of misfortune into Pim's clean white ear, "that I have never deliberately killed a woman in my life."

And then Guerin heard Pim murmur quietly in her stiff polite way, as if she were interviewing some well-meaning but unfortunate backsliding parishioner in the Deanery: "I'm so glad to hear it." And then the fiend out of hell, incarnate in the sewer rat with the angel face, fell back on his pillows with a sudden look of sharp self-disgust, and Pim moved off down the ward about her business.

I don't think it occurred to her to wonder what his phrase implied, or how many women he had killed, as he would have called it, by accident, or how many men with intent. I don't believe she was aware of the immense compliment he had paid her, or of having gained any victory over him. She had no knowledge of vice or evil. She did not know that he was truly one of the damned, and that his heart was black and heavy with a sick black weight of fear that came sweeping over him in his new weakness, and so next day, when he began to be frightened, she was surprised by the wild gleams of fear that came and went in his eyes.

But Guerin knew. He was a student of men, and he knew that the Enfant de Malheur was his brother, and believed in what he himself believed, namely, in the Holy Catholic Church and the Life Everlasting, in God, and the Mother of God, and the Holy Son of God, against whom he had fought and blasphemed since the day he was born.

His condition, both physical and moral, grew rapidly worse after this. Symptoms of gangrene set in. A second amputation was necessary, high up the thigh, almost at the hip, and again Pim, who had followed her patient to the operating room, was told to go away. She refused. She stood there obstinately while streams of filth and obscenity spurted from his beautiful pale mouth—putrid psychic sewage of the underworld spouting from him like a fountain; but to the surgeon's embarrassed, irritated excuses she answered: "I don't understand his language, so what difference does it make?" and she took him back and put him gently to bed.

But when he came to after the operation, there was a new look in his eyes. Pim went white at the sight of it, and her hand, as she put the long saline needle into his side, trembled, and she went in search of Guerin.

"He is so frightened," she said, "he is so afraid to die. I can't bear it. We must save him, Guerin."

So they conspired to save him. There were forty beds in the hut, and they were all full; but those two—Pim and Guerin—

without fuss multiplied themselves. No royal patient was ever
nursed with greater care than our Enfant de Malheur, but he
grew worse, and his fear grew worse. His fear increased until
its presence filled the ward, and the old greybeards in their
beds turned away their faces and stopped their ears to hide
from it.

He began to sweat terribly. He began to toss and writhe. He
began to smell bad. Moods of blasphemous bravado alternated
with fits of uncontrollable panic. In the middle of a curse his
teeth would begin to chatter. Then suddenly his eyes would
start from his head in terror, and he would shriek for help and
thrash out wildly till Pim came to him or Guerin. Sometimes
he sobbed like a child in Pim's arms. More often he raged at
her, cursed her and Guerin and God. His bed became a center
of obscenity. Foul odours, foul words, foul matter swirled
round him, and always there was that terror in his eyes, and
the sweat pouring down his body that was greenish now as if
covered with slime. The tattooed lady smiled through the slime
on his back, and he would wave his wasted arm and hit out
with it, and the big letters seemed to shout to Pim down the
ward: Enfant de Malheur!

Finally he could not bear her near him, could not bear the
sight of her near his bed or the touch of her hands. One afternoon he yelled at her to go away, leave him alone. She had
maintained so far her stolid serenity but at that she broke
down. I found her behind her screen at the end of the ward
with her shoulders shaking, her face twisting. It was nine
o'clock in the evening. I told her to go off duty at once.

"But he is going to die in the night," she whispered.

"I know."

"And he is terribly frightened."

"I know."

"His fear is so ugly. It frightens me and the others, all the old men. We must do something. Can't we do something?"

"Perhaps Guerin can do something. You and I, what can we do?"

"If only he weren't so sane. If only he didn't realise. But his fever seems to have sharpened his wits. He knows he is going to die. He never forgets for a second. He hasn't had a wink of sleep. Dying usually slows down, blurs everything, brings a merciful dullness; but for him there is no such mercy. His nerves are live wires. Morphine has no effect. I've given him extra doses. No good, not a bit of good. But he must have relief, I tell you. This is impossible." Her face had a slightly crazed look. "I tell you I am ready to give him any amount of stuff. I'll do anything to put an end to it."

I said, "Come along, Pim. You can't kill your patient. Come now at once. You're doing no good here." What he wants, I said to myself, is to be convinced that he has nothing to be afraid of. But suppose I tried to convince him that there was nothing to fear, no God, no crucified Christ waiting, no everlasting life stretching ahead of him, nothing but nothingness, I could never convince him—never. I had no power over his fear.

Guerin met me at the door of the hut as I was going out with Pim. He was polishing his eyeglasses.

"I would like permission to spend the night in the ward," he said in his quick way, adjusting his pince-nez on his pointed nose.

"Very well, Guerin. You've been on duty all day, and you'll be on all day to-morrow, remember."

"Don't worry about that," he said briefly, dismissing us both with a wave of his hand.

"Can I do nothing, Guerin?" Pim asked meekly.

"Nothing, Mademoiselle."

They looked at each other. Then she looked down the ward to where the boy was lying and her mouth contracted. We could distinguish from our distance the terrified eyes.

"What is he afraid of?" she asked, shuddering.

"Of hell, Mademoiselle," said Guerin. And suddenly, as if he had heard us, some power jerked the boy off his pillow, and his arms shot out in front of him. "Je ne meurs pas," he cried; "Je ne meurs pas. Je ne voudrais pas mourir." I hurried Pim away.

When I went back, Guerin was on his knees by the boy's bed reading in low rapid tones from a little book. The Enfant de Malheur was not listening. He was quite unaware of him. He was entirely and horribly absorbed by another presence that seemed to be attacking him as an octopus attacks with many arms. He was writhing in the unseen clutches. He was dodging and twisting and hissing at the thing through clenched teeth, and his eyes darted this way and that like beings separate from himself, possessed by a panic of their own.

I went from bed to bed attending to the old grumbling ones and trying not to look, but I could hear his fear increasing. Its tempo grew audibly more rapid, more frantic. His invisible en-

emy seemed to be going for him now in rushes and leaps of increasing fury. I hurried through my work, scolding in whispers
the old men who were annoyed by his noise and troubled by his
fear. I rattled my basins and kettles, making a noise of my own
to distract them. But I could hear the boy's sobbing breath,
hear him choking and shuddering, and every few seconds his
voice would burst from his suffocating chest in a wail of
defiant terror, and once he went off into a peal of hysterical
laughter.

Guerin's low voice went on through it all. His words followed each other rapidly, in a monotone, in a level directed
chant. He was aiming them straight at the head of the sweat-
ing terror-struck creature beside him. He paid no attention to
me. Neither of them was aware of me. I hurried past them and
went out.

I had a great deal to do. I went from hut to hut. I gave
piqûres and medicines and drinks, adjusted bandages and pillows, filled hot water bottles. I busied myself, making an unnecessary fuss over my duties, and tried to absorb myself in re-
lieving the shadowy suffering forms that lay so patiently,
murmuring their gratitude. I was greedy for their gratitude. I
wanted badly to be comforted. But I had a feeling of sickening
suspense and miserable futility. I could not forget those two.
But I thought of them as three. I caught myself saying to myself: "There is Guerin and the Enfant de Malheur and another.
It isn't just a case of one man fighting the panic of another.
That's what you call it. That's what you want to believe it is.
But there is something there that inspires the panic. Some-

thing else, something immense. The boy is a worm; the priest is an insignificant little man. But there are huge invisible things assaulting that noisome bed. What? The powers of darkness?"

"Nonsense," I said to myself. I was adjusting the pulleys of a fracture case. "There are no dark powers abroad in the world. There is only death and pain and human evil and puny human remorse. The boy is a murderer, a thief, a vile rat, and he knows it; that's all, but soon it will all be over. Soon he'll be nothing, nothing. You know all the rest is silly superstition. If Guerin didn't happen to be a Catholic priest he wouldn't take it so hard."

But even the quiet huts full of sleeping men seemed to be filled with mystery, and I hurried to get back to that other one across the way, where I knew an immense struggle was going on. I couldn't bear not to see what was happening. I was afraid to go back, but fascinated, haunted, allured. "If Guerin didn't happen to be a priest he would be as useless as you are in the face of this," I said to myself. But could even Guerin do anything? Who was Guerin? A good orderly, a conscientious little man who believed in old legends. Very well, very well. Put it that the power of an aged belief was being put to the test in that ugly hut. I must see; I must know. I was devoured with curiosity.

My round took me two hours. It was midnight when I got back to them. Guerin was in the same position, on his knees, but he was praying now with a crucifix in his lifted hands and his eyes were closed. His face showed signs of great fatigue; it was tight and strained, but it wore a curious expression. And this expression was so concentrated that it seemed to come from his face and shoot upward like a shaft of dark light. I cannot describe it otherwise. His voice, too, had gained in power; it was low, level, and penetrating, but there were undertones in it that made one's nerves tingle. "Dieu qui nous regarde, ayez pitié. Dieu le Sauveur, je vous supplie——"

The Enfant de Malheur, I saw with a sickening catch in my side, had changed too, and the change was dreadful. I had hoped. What had I hoped? In his growing exhaustion and terror he had a look of madness. He was almost unrecognisable. There was a devilish hatred on his clammy face, a vile frantic fury, as well as an agony of terror. His fury seemed directed toward Guerin and the crucifix, while his terror was concentrated on something straight in front of him. His lips were twisted into a malevolent and hideous snarl; his eyes were the eyes of a suffering lunatic; they shot sullen sidelong looks of wild vindictiveness at the crucifix. As I passed he gave a vicious leap toward the foot of the bed, flung his tortured body past the priest's head, hit out at the Christ with his fist, and, grinding his teeth, yelled out a hideous curse into the shadows. Guerin's voice became audible again an instant later: "Dieu, notre seul espoir—Dieu, notre Sauveur." The old men groaned and muttered, half waking.

At two o'clock the struggle was still going on and the situation seemed to me at first unchanged except that the apache and the priest were both fainting with exhaustion; but I noticed presently that they had come to closer grips with each other. Guerin, still on his knees, was talking now with his mouth close to the boy's head, talking with a breathless intensity, saying apparently the same thing over and over, as if he were trying to drive home into that maddened brain a single important fact, and it seemed to me that through his terror the dying boy was listening in spite of himself. His attention was now very evidently divided between the death that menaced him at the foot of his bed and the voice that spoke in his ear. He was still fighting, but while he fought he listened reluctantly, fearful of allowing his attention to be distracted from his awful antagonist for a second, but nevertheless compelled to pay attention. And his antagonist seemed to have withdrawn a little. The beast was crouching, was cowering now, so it seemed to me. I stood at a distance under the lamp that hung from the peaked roof and watched. Guerin was panting for breath as if he had been running in a long race. But he seemed to be winning: he seemed to have pushed back a little that dark power. The boy was undoubtedly listening to his rapid, determined, insistent voice. The power in it was reaching him. What power? Guerin's, you fool, I said to myself, but what powers did Guerin have to draw on. He had been at it now for four hours. Could he last out, keep it up? Keep up what? What, after all, was he doing? Was he telling the sewer rat lies to get him quiet? But how could he go on lying and lying? What power lay in tricks and falsehood to rout that awful terror? If Guerin failed he would, I caught myself thinking, be proved a liar; but if he won, what then? And just at that moment I saw the boy break away from Guerin's voice and plunge with a shriek back into his agony and begin to writhe again as if grappling with a monster; and I almost ran to the door, sick with horror and disappointment.

"He has failed," I said to myself. "Guerin has failed." And I hurried away with my lantern through the bitter air, making excuses for him. "It's too long, it's too much. He's been at it all night. No man on earth could keep it up at that pitch of intensity." I stopped, stood staring down at my lantern. "But he'd almost got him," I whispered, "and now he's lost him again." But had he? I turned round. Suppose Guerin had given up? I went running back. "I couldn't bear that, Guerin," I whispered. "I couldn't bear to see you beaten"; I felt half suffocated as I crept to the door and looked in again.

Guerin had not relaxed or changed his position; he was still praying, praying. His words came to my ears like the soft raps of a small muffled hammer, hammering away, hammering and hammering.

And as I went on my rounds again, from hut to hut and bed to bed, I kept hearing Guerin's voice, hammering away, hammering away at the gates of Heaven for the sake of the poor Enfant de Malheur. I knew now that nothing could stop him, that he would never give in, but I knew, too, that his time was getting short. The boy couldn't last much longer. Soon he would die. Would he die in terror, aware of his unutterable vileness? Would Guerin be forced to see that happen? Would he be proved to himself to be a liar?

I felt cold and very tired. The sky was beginning to pale. It was four o'clock, the hour when life beats most feebly in the bodies of men. I went from hut to hut again, listening for the little sounds of uncertain fluttering life. Was this one slipping away or that one? "No one, no one else must die to-night," I kept saying to myself. "There is only one death here to-night." Then I turned toward Guerin's hut. It stood ungainly and ugly in the half light, a wooden shelter through which many men had passed, some to go home, some to be buried in our cemetery where the wooden crosses stood so modestly above the ground. None of them stayed with us. All were lost to us. They passed like shadows. I could not remember them. They had no names, no faces in my memory. Who were they? What were they? What had become of them? I did not know. I knew nothing about them; I knew nothing of the dead or the living. I felt cold. I felt dreadfully cold as I approached the door, but as I entered I was aware that a strange hush had come into the ward, and through it I heard the old men breathing, and a young voice talking. It was the Enfant de Malheur who was speaking. He was talking to Guerin in a small weak child's voice, and Guerin was kneeling beside him with the sweat pouring down his face. I saw Guerin take his handkerchief from his pocket and wipe his forehead, but he did not take his eyes from the boy's eyes while he did this. They were both quiet; Guerin was very, very quiet, but the boy was sobbing a little. He was confessing his sins. He was pouring out all his dark, secret, haunting memories into Guerin's ears and sobbing with relief. I turned and tip-toed out again, and stood for a while against the wall of the hut, trembling. I went back at five. I could not keep away. I went back half through my round.

The Forbidden Zone

I knew that I must not miss the last act of the drama that was playing itself out so quietly on that ugly narrow bed. I knew that I would never again in this world see anything so mysterious.

The dawn was filtering into the long wooden hut, filling it with the twilight of morning. The old men in their beds lay asleep. I looked down the long row apprehensively with a last catch at the heart. Was it over? Had Guerin really won? No, it was not over yet. Yes, yes, he had won. There they were, the two of them, and the boy's white face was smiling above smoothed sheets. His eyes were closed. He lay relaxed, at peace, happy, and a small crumpled figure was still kneeling beside his bed and a low voice was praying again: "Jésu— Dieu—Sauveur qui nous regarde." And I knew that the Enfant de Malheur was listening. I knew that he could hear, because he moved a little, and touched the priest's arm, half opened his eyes, and smiled as I watched him.

He died at six o'clock, holding Guerin by the hand. Then Guerin loosed his hand, and crossed the boy's two hands on his wasted chest over the small crucifix, and rose from his knees and walked stiffly to the door.

The sun was rising. He staggered a little as he came out into the fresh morning air. I stood beside him. He began polishing his pince-nez. The sky was crimson behind the wooden sheds. Suddenly, softly, it filled with golden light. Great luminous bands spread up and out like a fan from the horizon. I looked at Guerin, so small, so crumpled, so exhausted. He did not look at all like a man of God. He looked like a bookworm, a bit of a prig, an insignificant little man.

"What does it mean, Guerin?" I asked. "It was like a miracle; but what does it mean?"

"He is safe." Guerin said briefly. Then he adjusted his pince-nez, gave me a quick sharp look, and turned away to his own quarters.

Rosa

❦

THE STRETCHER BEARERS staggered under his weight
when they brought him along through the sunlight to
the operating room. They put him down for a moment
on the ground outside the operating hut and wiped the sweat
off their old foreheads. It was a hot summer's day. The sector
was quiet. The attack that had filled the hospital two days before had fizzled out. Now only occasional ambulances lurched
in at the gate, bringing men who had been missed by the
stretcher bearers, left out for a couple of nights on No Man's
Land, or been wounded unnecessarily by stray bullets after the
big push was over. This man had come up over the horizon
alone, a red giant, brought unconscious through the summer
afternoon in a battered Ford, and deposited like a log on our
doorstep, solitary character of some obscure incident in the af-
termath of battle. He lay on the ground like a felled ox, a bull
mortally wounded, breathing noisily.

His head was bound with a soiled bandage; his eyes were
closed; his bruised mouth was open. Thick tufts of red hair
pushed through the head bandage. There was dried blood
round his immense rough lips. His huge red face was dark and
blurred. He was covered with dust. He looked as if he had been

rolling in a dirty field like some farm animal. He was a man of the soil, of the dark earth, with the heavy power of the earth in him. The bright sun shining on his massive unconscious bulk made the darkness of his lost consciousness visible. He seemed to lie deep, distant, withdrawn in a shadowy abyss. His spirit—brother spirit of ox and bullock and all beasts of the field—was deep asleep, in that sleep which is the No Man's Land of the soul, and from which men seldom come back. But his immense body continued, in spite of his absence to hum and drum like a dynamo, like a machine whose tremendous power takes time to run down, and his breath came whistling and spurting through his rough bruised lips like escaping steam.

The old stretcher-bearers lifted him again grunting, and brought him in to us and hoisted him with difficulty on to the narrow white table, in the white room full of glistening bottles and shining basins and silvered instruments, among the white-coated surgeons and nurses. His head hung over one end of the table, and his feet over the other, and his great freckled arms hung helpless and heavy down at either side. Thick curling bunches of red hair, wiry and vigorous, grew out of his enormous chest. We stripped his body. It lay inert, a mountain-ous mass, with the rough-hewn brick-red face tipped back. His sightless face reminded one of the face of a rock in a sandstone quarry, chiselled with a pick-axe, deeply gashed. His closed eyes were caves under bushy cliffs, his battered mouth a dark shaft leading down into a cavern where a hammer was beating.

Because he was so big, his helplessness was the more helpless. But one could feel life pounding powerfully in his body—senseless life, pounding on, pumping air into his lungs, keeping his heart going. Yes, he would be hard to kill, I thought. Even a bullet in the head hadn't killed him.

I counted his pulse. It was strong and steady.

"Shot through the mouth. Revolver bullet lodged in the brain." Monsieur X was reading the ticket that had been pinned to the man's blanket in the dressing station behind the front line.

But how? I wondered. How queer, I thought. Shot in the mouth—through the roof of the mouth. He must have been asleep in the trench with his mouth open. And I imagined him there, sprawling in the muddy ditch, an exhausted animal with his great stupid mouth open; and I saw a figure crawl in beside him and put the barrel of a revolver between his big yellow teeth. Fool, I thought. You fool—you big hulking brute beast—going to sleep like that in utter careless weariness.

But no, it was impossible. In this war such things didn't happen. Men were killed haphazard—maimed, torn to pieces, scattered by shell fire, plugged full of shrapnel, hit square sometimes by rifle bullets, but not shot neatly through the roof of the mouth with a revolver.

They were whispering as they bent over him. Monsieur X frowned, pinched his lips together, looked down at the great, gentle unconscious carcase sideways.

"But how?" I asked. "Who?"

"Himself. He shot himself through the mouth. It's a suicide."

The Forbidden Zone

"Suicide!" I echoed the word vaguely, as if it contained a mystery. There was something queer, out of the ordinary, about it, shocking to the surgeons and orderlies. They were ashamed, worried, rather flustered. "But why suicide?" I asked, suddenly aware of the extraordinary fact that a personal tragedy had lifted its head above the dead level of mass destruction. It was this that shocked them.

He's not young, I thought, cutting the bandage round the rough unconscious head with its shock of matted red hair. A peasant, probably—very stupid—an ox of a man.

"Why suicide?" I asked aloud.

"Panic," answered Monsieur briefly. "Fear—he tried to kill himself from fear of being killed. They do sometimes."

"This one didn't."

"No, he didn't succeed, this big one. He ought to be dead. The bullet is here just under the skull. It's gone clean through his brain. Any other man would be dead. He's strong, this big one."

"You'll extract it?"

"But certainly."

"And he will live?"

"Perhaps."

"And what then?"

"He'll be court-martialed and shot, Madame, for attempted suicide."

They were strapping his iron arms and legs to the narrow table. Someone lifted his heavy head. Someone pulled his great bulk into position and bound him to the table with strong leather bands.

"Don't do it!" I shouted suddenly. "Leave him alone." I was appalled by his immense helplessness.

They went on with their business of getting him ready. They didn't hear me. Perhaps I had not shouted aloud.

"You don't understand," I cried. "You've made a mistake. It wasn't fear. It was something else. He had a reason, a secret. It's locked there in his chest. Leave him alone with it. You can't bring him back now to be shot again."

But they clapped the ether mask over his face, stifling his enormous stertorous breathing, and with that he began to struggle—the dying ox. Life, roused by the menace of the suffocating gas, sprang up in him again—gigantic, furious, suffering, a baited bull. It began plunging in him, straining, leaping to get out of his carcase and attack its enemies. A leather thong snapped, a fist shot out, knocking over bottles and basins. There was a crash, a tinkle of broken glass, a scramble of feet, and suddenly through the confusion I heard a thin soft anguished voice cry as if from a great distance, "Rosa, Rosa!" It came from his chest; it sounded like the voice of a man lost in a cave. It came from under his heaving side where the bushy hair grew thick and strong—a hollow heartbroken voice, issuing from his blind unconscious mouth, in a long cry—"Rosa, Rosa!"

Twice again he called Rosa before they could clap the ether mask down again on his face.

The Forbidden Zone

It was a neat operation and entirely successful. They took the bullet out of the top of his head, bandaged his head up again, and carried him away through the sunny afternoon to be put to bed.

"He will surely die in the night," I said to myself, and I went again and again in the night to see if, happily, he were dead; but always, standing beside the shadow of his great bulk, I could hear him breathing, and once I thought I heard sighing on his shrouded lips the name of the woman—Rosa.

"He can't live," the night nurse said.

"He can't die," I whispered to myself. "Life is too strong in him, too hard to kill."

He was much better next day. I found him sitting up in bed in a clean pink flannel night shirt, staring in front of him. He didn't answer when I said "Good morning," or take any notice of me. He hadn't spoken to any one during the day, the nurse told me, but he was very obedient and ate his soup quietly, "as good as gold," she said he was. "A remarkable case," Monsieur X said. "He ought to be dead." But there he was sitting up eating his meals with an excellent appetite.

"So he knows what will happen?" I asked, following the surgeon to the door.

"But certainly. They all know. Everyone in the army knows the penalty."

The suicide did not turn his head or look in my direction. He was still staring straight ahead of him when I came back and stood at the foot of his bed.

Who are you? I wondered, and who is Rosa? And what can I

{ 124 }

do? How can I help you? And I stood there waiting, miserably spellbound by the patient brute who at last turned on me from his cavernous eyes a look of complete understanding, and then looked heavily away again.

That night when the orderly was dozing and the night nurse was going on her round from hut to hut, he tore the bandage from his head. She found him with his head oozing on the pillow, and scolded him roundly. He didn't answer. He said nothing. He seemed not to notice. Meekly, docile as a friendly trusting dog, he let her bandage him up again, and the next morning I found him again sitting up in his bed in his clean head bandage staring in front of him with that dark look of dumb subhuman suffering. And the next night the same thing happened, and the next, and the next. Every night he tore off his bandage, and then let himself be tied up again.

"If his wound becomes infected he'll die," said Monsieur X, angrily.

"That's what he's trying to do," I answered. "Kill himself again before they can shoot him," I added, "to save them the trouble."

I dared not speak to the man whom I thought of day and night as Rosa, having never learned his name, and he never spoke to me or any one. His eyes, which he now always turned on me when I came in, forbade me to speak to him. They stared into mine with the understanding of a brute mortally wounded, who is not allowed to die, so I went to the General, and, actuated by some hysterical impulse, pleaded for the man's life.

The Forbidden Zone

"But, Madame, we have epidemics of suicide in the trenches. Panic seizes the men. They blow their brains out in a panic. Unless the penalty is what it is—to be court-martialed and shot—the thing would spread. We'd find ourselves going over the top with battalions of dead men. The same penalty applies to men who wound themselves. That's the favourite device of a coward. He puts the muzzle of his rifle on his foot and fires."

I argued. I explained that this man was not afraid of being killed, but of not being killed, that his luck was out when the enemy missed him; that he had been kept waiting too long, had shot himself in despair because the Germans wouldn't shoot him; and a woman called Rosa let him down, or perhaps she died. Perhaps he simply wanted to go to her.

"He must have had a letter in the trenches—a letter from Rosa or about her. He's not a young man. He is forty or more—an enormous brute with red hair and hands like hams. A farmer probably. One of those slow plodding gentle brute men, faithful as dogs. His voice was broken-hearted, high and hollow like a child's voice, when he called to her. Like a child that is lost. 'Rosa! Rosa!' If you'd heard him.

"And here you are with your military regulations asking me to save him for you so that you can shoot him. You expect us to tie up his head every night and prevent his dying so that you can march him off to trial and stand him up against a wall."

But what was the good of arguing against army regulations? We were at war. The General could do nothing. The man must be made an example, so that these epidemics of suicide could be kept in check.

I didn't dare go back to Rosa. I went to the door of the hut and called the nurse. Down in the centre of the long row of beds I could see Rosa's great shoulders and his huge bandaged head. He looked like a monstrous baby in his white bonnet and pink flannel shirt. But I knew that his big haggard eyes were staring, and I remembered that his face had been a little paler each day, that it was not brick colour any more, but the colour of wax, that his cheek bones stood out like shelves.

He's killing himself in spite of us all, I thought. He's succeeding. It's hard work, it takes patience, but he's doing it. Given a chance, he'll pull it off. Well, he'll have his chance. I almost laughed. I had been a fool to go to the General and plead for his life. That was the last thing he wanted me to do for him. That was just the wrong thing.

I spoke to the nurse who was going on duty for the night.

"When Rosa pulls off his bandage tonight, leave it off," I said abruptly.

She looked at me a minute hesitating. She was highly trained. Her traditions, her professional conscience, the honour of her calling loomed for a moment before her, then her eyes lighted. "All right," she said.

I thought when I stood at the foot of Rosa's bed next morning and found him staring at me that I detected a look of recognition in his eyes, perhaps even a faint look of gratitude, but I could not be sure. His gaze was so sombre, so deep, that I could not read it, but I could see that he was weaker. Perhaps it was his increased pallor that made his eyes so enormously dark and mysterious. Toward evening he grew delirious, but he tore off his bandage all the same, in the middle of the night. He managed to do that. It was his last effort, his last fumbling desperate and determined act. His fixed idea prevailed through his delirium, his will triumphed. It was enough. He was unconscious next morning and he died two days later, calling in his weary abysmal heart for Rosa, though we could not hear him.

Conspiracy

❧

IT IS ALL carefully arranged. Everything is arranged. It is
arranged that men should be broken and that they should
be mended. Just as you send your clothes to the laundry
and mend them when they come back, so we send our men to
the trenches and mend them when they come back again. You
send your socks and your shirts again and again to the laundry,
and you sew up the tears and clip the ravelled edges again and
again just as many times as they will stand it. And then you
throw them away. And we send our men to the war again and
again, just as long as they will stand it; just until they are dead,
and then we throw them into the ground.

It is all arranged. Ten kilometres from here along the road is
the place where men are wounded. This is the place where
they are mended. We have all the things here for mending, the
tables and the needles, and the thread and the knives and the
scissors, and many curious things that you never use for your
clothes.

We bring our men up along the dusty road where the bushes
grow on either side and the green trees. They come by in the
mornings in companies, marching with strong legs, with firm
steps. They carry their knapsacks easily. Their knapsacks and

their guns and their greatcoats are not heavy for them. They wear their caps jauntily, tilted to one side. Their faces are ruddy and their eyes bright. They smile and call out with strong voices. They throw kisses to the girls in the fields.

We send our men up the broken road between bushes of barbed wire and they come back to us, one by one, two by two in ambulances, lying on stretchers. They lie on their backs on the stretchers and are pulled out of the ambulances as loaves of bread are pulled out of the oven. The stretchers slide out of the mouths of the ambulances with the men on them. The men cannot move. They are carried into a shed, unclean bundles, very heavy, covered with brown blankets.

We receive these bundles. We pull off a blanket. We observe that this is a man. He makes feeble whining sounds like an animal. He lies still; he smells bad; he smells like a corpse; he can only move his tongue; he tries to moisten his lips with his tongue.

This is the place where he is to be mended. We lift him on to a table. We peel off his clothes, his coat and his shirt and his trousers and his boots. We handle his clothes that are stiff with blood. We cut off his shirt with large scissors. We stare at the obscene sight of his innocent wounds. He allows us to do this. He is helpless to stop us. We wash off the dry blood round the edges of his wounds. He suffers us to do as we like with him. He says no word except that he is thirsty and we do not give him to drink.

We confer together over his body and he hears us. We discuss his different parts in terms that he does not understand, but he listens while we make calculations with his heart beats and the pumping breath of his lungs.

We conspire against his right to die. We experiment with his bones, his muscles, his sinews, his blood. We dig into the yawning mouths of his wounds. Helpless openings, they let us into the secret places of his body. We plunge deep into his body. We make discoveries within his body. To the shame of the havoc of his limbs we add the insult of our curiosity and the curse of our purpose, the purpose to remake him. We lay odds on his chances of escape, and we combat with Death, his saviour.

It is our business to do this. He knows and he allows us to do it. He finds himself in the operating room. He lays himself out. He bares himself to our knives. His mind is annihilated. He pours out his blood, unconscious. His red blood is spilled and pours over the table on to the floor while he sleeps.

After this, while he is still asleep, we carry him into another place and put him to bed. He awakes bewildered as children do, expecting, perhaps, to find himself at home with his mother leaning over him, and he moans a little and then lies still again. He is helpless, so we do for him what he cannot do for himself, and he is grateful. He accepts his helplessness. He is obedient. We feed him, and he eats. We fatten him up, and he allows himself to be fattened. Day after day he lies there and we watch him. All day and all night he is watched. Every day his wounds are uncovered and cleaned, scraped and washed and bound up again. His body does not belong to him. It belongs to us for the moment, not for long. He knows why we tend it so carefully. He knows what we are fattening and cleaning it up for; and while we handle it he smiles.

He is only one among thousands. They are all the same. They all let us do with them what we like. They all smile as if they were grateful. When we hurt them they try not to cry out, not wishing to hurt our feelings. And often they apologise for dying. They would not die and disappoint us if they could help it. Indeed, in their helplessness they do the best they can to help us get them ready to go back again.

It is only ten kilometres up the road, the place where they go to be torn again and mangled. Listen; you can hear how well it works. There is the sound of cannon and the sound of the ambulances bringing the wounded, and the sound of the tramp of strong men going along the road to fill the empty places.

Do you hear? Do you understand? It is all arranged just as it should be.

Paraphernalia

◦Υ◦

WHAT HAVE all these queer things to do with the dying of this man?

Here are cotton things and rubber things and steel things and things made of glass, all manner of things. What have so many things to do with the final adventure of this spirit?

Here are blankets and pillows and tin boxes and needles and bottles and pots and basins and long rubber tubes and many little white squares of gauze. Here are bottles of all sizes filled with coloured liquids and basins of curious shapes and round shining boxes and square boxes marked with blue labels, and here you are busy among your things. You pile the blankets on his exhausted body. You fetch jugs of hot water and boil the long curling rubber tubes in saucepans. You keep corking and uncorking bottles.

Yes, I know that you understand all these things. You finger the glass syringes exquisitely and pick up the fine needles easily with slender pincers and with the glass beads poised neatly on your rosy finger tips you saw them with tiny saws. You flaunt your perfect movements in the face of his mysterious exhaustion. You show off the skilled movements of your hands beside the erratic jerkings of his terrible limbs.

Why do you rub his grey flesh with the stained scrap of cotton and stick the needle deep into his side? Why do you do it?

Death is inexorable and the place of death is void. You have crowded the room with all manner of things. Why do you crowd all these things up to the edge of the great emptiness?

You seem to have so much to do. Wait. Wait. A miracle is going to happen. Death is coming into the room. There is no time for all this business. There is only one moment between this man and eternity.

You still fuss about busily. You move your feet and rustle your petticoats. You are continually doing things with your hands. You keep on doing things. Why do you keep on doing things? Death is annoyed at your fussing.

The man's spirit is invisible. Why do you light the lamp? You cannot see the God of Death with your splendid eyes. Does it please you to see the sweat on that forehead and the glaze on the eyeballs?

Hush, you are making a noise. Why do you make a noise? No, as you say, he cannot hear you, but cannot you hear? Eternity is soundless, but hush! Let us listen. Let us listen. Maybe we shall hear the stirring of wings or the sighing tremor of his soul passing.

Ah! What are you doing? Why do you move? You are filling the room with sound as you have filled it with objects. You are annoying Death with your ridiculous things and the noise of your foolish business.

Paraphernalia

What do you say? He is dead? You say he is dead?

And here are all your things, your blankets and your bottles and your basins. The blankets weigh down upon his body. They hang down over the bed. Your syringes and your needles and your uncorked bottles are all about in confusion. You have stained your fingers. There is a spot on your white apron; but you are superb, and here are all your things about you, all your queer things, all the confusion of your precious things.

What have you and all your things to do with the dying of this man? Nothing. Take them away.

In the Operating Room

❧

THE OPERATING ROOM is the section of a wooden shed. Thin partitions separate it from the X-ray room on one side, and the sterilizing room on the other. Another door communicates with a corridor. There are three wounded men on three operating tables. Surgeons, nurses and orderlies are working over them. The doors keep opening and shutting. The boiler is pounding and bubbling in the sterilizing room. There is a noise of steam escaping, of feet hurrying down the corridor, of ambulances rolling past the windows, and behind all this, the rhythmic pounding of the guns bombarding at a distance of ten miles or so.

1st Patient: Mother of God! Mother of God!

2nd Patient: Softly. Softly. You hurt me. Ah! You are hurting me.

3rd Patient: I am thirsty.

1st Surgeon: Cut the dressing, Mademoiselle.

2nd Surgeon: What's his ticket say? Show it to me. What's the X-ray show?

3rd Surgeon: Abdomen. Bad pulse. I wonder now?

1st Patient: In the name of God be careful. I suffer. I suffer.

1st Surgeon: At what time were you wounded?

1st Patient: At five this morning.

1st Surgeon: Where?

1st Patient: In the arm.

1st Surgeon: Yes, yes, but in what sector?

1st Patient: In the trenches near Besanghe.

1st Surgeon: Shell or bullet?

1st Patient: Shell. Merciful God, what are you doing?

A nurse comes in from the corridor. Her apron is splashed with blood.

Nurse: There's a lung just come in. Hæmorrhage. Can one of you take him?

1st Surgeon: In a few minutes. In five minutes. Now then, Mademoiselle, strap down that other arm tighter.

Nurse (in doorway) to 2nd Surgeon: There's a knee for you, doctor, and three elbows. In five minutes I'll send in the lung. (Exit.)

3rd Patient: I'm thirsty. A drink. Give me a drink.

3rd Surgeon: In a little while. You must wait a little.

2nd Patient: Mother of Jesus, not like that. Don't turn my foot like that. Not that way. Take care. Great God, take care! I can't bear it. I tell you, I can't bear it!

2nd Surgeon: There, there, don't excite yourself. You've got a nasty leg, very nasty. Smells bad. Mademoiselle, hold his leg up. It's not pretty at all, this leg.

2nd Patient: Ah, doctor, doctor. What are you doing? Aiee ——.

2nd Surgeon: Be quiet. Don't move. Don't touch the wound,

In the Operating Room

I tell you. Idiot! Hold his leg. Keep your hands off, you animal. Hold his leg higher. Strap his hands down.

3rd Patient (feebly): I am thirsty. I die of thirst. A drink! A drink!

2nd Patient (screaming): You're killing me. Killing me! I'll die of it! Aieeeee——.

3rd Patient (softly): I am thirsty. For pity a drink.

3rd Surgeon: Have you vomited blood, old man?

3rd Patient: I don't know. A drink please, doctor.

3rd Surgeon: Does it hurt here?

3rd Patient: No, I don't think so. A drink, sister, in pity's name, a drink.

Nurse: I can't give you a drink. It would hurt you. You are wounded in the stomach.

3rd Patient: So thirsty. Just a little drink. Just a drop. Sister for pity, just a drop.

3rd Surgeon: Moisten his lips. How long ago were you wounded?

3rd Patient: I don't know. In the night. Some night.

3rd Surgeon: Last night?

3rd Patient: Perhaps last night. I don't know. I lay in the mud a long time. Please, sister, a drink. Just a little drink.

1st Patient: What's in that bottle? What are you doing to me?

1st Surgeon: Keep still I tell you.

1st Patient: It burns! It's burning me! No more. No more! I beg of you, doctor; I can't bear any more!

1st Surgeon: Nonsense. This won't last a minute. There's nothing the matter with you. Your wounds are nothing.

{ 139 }

1st Patient: You say it's nothing. My God, what are you doing now? Ai—ee!

1st Surgeon: It's got to be cleaned out. There's a piece of shell, bits of coat, all manner of dirt in it.

2nd Patient: Jeanne, petite Marie, Jean, where are you? Little Jean, where are you?

2nd Surgeon: Your leg is not at all pretty, my friend. We shall have to take it off.

2nd Patient: Oh, my poor wife? I have three children, doctor. If you take my leg off what will become of them and of the farm? Great God, to suffer like this!

2nd Surgeon to 1st Surgeon: Look here a moment. It smells bad. Gangrenous. What do you think?

1st Surgeon: No good waiting.

2nd Surgeon: Well, my friend, will you have it off?

2nd Patient: If you say so, doctor. Oh, my poor wife, my poor Jeanne. What will become of you? The children are too little to work in the fields.

2nd Surgeon (to nurse): Begin with the chloroform. We're going to put you to sleep, old man. Breathe deep. Breathe through the mouth. Is my saw there? Where is my amputating saw? Who's got my saw?

3rd Patient (softly): A drink, a drink. Give me a drink.

3rd Surgeon: I can do nothing with a pulse like that. Give him serum, five hundred c.c.s. and camphorated oil and strychnine. Warm him up a bit.

Door opens, nurse enters, followed by two stretcher bearers.

Nurse: Here's the lung. Are you ready for it?

In the Operating Room

1st Surgeon: In a minute. One minute. Leave him there.

The stretcher bearers put their stretcher on the floor and go out.

2nd Patient (half under chloroform): Aha! Aha! Ahead there, you son of a——. Forward! Forward! What a stink! I've got him! Now I've got you. Quick, quick! Let me go! Let me go! Jeannette, quick, quick, Jeannette! I'm coming. Marie? Little Jean, where are you?

2nd Surgeon: Tighten those straps. He's strong, poor devil.

1st Patient: Is it finished?

1st Surgeon: Very nearly. Keep quite still. Now then, the dressings, Mademoiselle. There you are, old man. Don't bandage the arm too tight, Mademoiselle. Get him out now. Hi, stretcher bearers, lift up that one from the floor, will you?

3rd Surgeon: It's no use operating. Almost no pulse.

3rd Patient: For pity a drink!

3rd Surgeon: Give him a drink. It won't matter. I can do nothing.

2nd Surgeon: I shall have to amputate above the knee. Is he under?

Nurse: Almost.

3rd Patient: For pity a drink.

Nurse: There, don't lift your head; here is a drink. Drink this.

3rd Patient: It is good. Thank you, sister.

1st Surgeon: Take this man to Ward 3. Now and then, Mademoiselle, cut the dressings.

3rd Surgeon: I can do nothing here. Send me the next one.

3rd Patient: I cannot see. I cannot see any more. Sister, where are you?

1st Surgeon: How's your spine case of yesterday?

3rd Surgeon: Just what you would expect—paralysed from the waist down.

1st Surgeon: They say the attack is for five in the morning.

3rd Surgeon: Orders are to evacuate every possible bed to-day.

3rd Patient: It is dark. Are you there, sister?

Nurse: Yes, old man, I'm here. Shall I send for a priest, doctor?

3rd Surgeon: Too late. Poor devil. It's hopeless when they come in like that, after lying for hours in the mud. There, it's finished. Call the stretcher bearers.

1st Surgeon: Quick, a basin! God! how the blood spouts. Quick, quick, quick! Three holes in this lung.

2nd Surgeon: Take that leg away, will you? There's no room to move here.

3rd Surgeon: Take this dead man away, and bring the next abdomen. Wipe that table, Mademoiselle, while I wash my hands. And you, there, mop up the floor a bit.

The doors open and shut. Stretcher bearers go out and come in. A nurse comes from the sterilizing room with a pile of nickel drums in her arms. Another nurse goes out with trays of knives and other instruments. The nurse from the corridor comes back. An officer appears at the window.

Nurse: Three knees have come in, two more abdomens, five heads.

In the Operating Room

Officer (through the window): The Médecin Inspecteur will be here in half an hour. The General is coming at two to decorate all amputés.

1st Surgeon: We'll get no lunch to-day, and I'm hungry. There, I call that a very neat amputation.

2nd Surgeon: Three holes stopped in this lung in three minutes by the clock. Pretty quick, eh?

3rd Surgeon: Give me a light, some one. My experience is that if abdomens have to wait more than six hours it's no good. You can't do anything. I hope that chap got the oysters in Amiens! Oysters sound good to me.

Blind

ⱽ

THE DOOR at the end of the baraque kept opening and shutting to let in the stretcher bearers. As soon as it opened a crack the wind scurried in and came hopping toward me across the bodies of the men that covered the floor, nosing under the blankets, lifting the flaps of heavy coats, and burrowing among the loose heaps of clothing and soiled bandages. Then the grizzled head of a stretcher bearer would appear, butting its way in, and he would emerge out of the black storm into the bright fog that seemed to fill the place, dragging the stretcher after him, and then the old one at the other end of the load would follow, and they would come slowly down the centre of the hut looking for a clear place on the floor.

The men were laid out in three rows on either side of the central alley way. It was a big hut, and there were about sixty stretchers in each row. There was space between the heads of one row and the feet of another row, but no space to pass between the stretchers in the same row; they touched. The old territorials who worked with me passed up and down between the heads and feet. I had a squad of thirty of these old orderlies and two sergeants and two priests, who were expert dressers. Wooden screens screened off the end of the hut opposite the entrance. Behind these were the two dressing tables where the priests dressed the wounds of the new arrivals and got them ready for the surgeons, after the old men had undressed them and washed their feet. In one corner was my kitchen where I kept all my syringes and hypodermic needles and stimulants.

It was just before midnight when the stretcher bearers brought in the blind man and there was no space on the floor anywhere; so they stood waiting, not knowing what to do with him.

I said from the floor in the second row: "Just a minute, old ones. You can put him here in a minute." So they waited with the blind man suspended in the bright, hot, misty air between them, like a pair of old horses in shafts with their heads down, while the little boy who had been crying for his mother died with his head on my breast. Perhaps he thought the arms holding him when he jerked back and died belonged to some woman I had never seen, some woman waiting somewhere for news of him in some village, somewhere in France. How many women, I wondered, were waiting out there in the distance for news of these men who were lying on the floor? But I stopped thinking about this the minute the boy was dead. It didn't do to think. I didn't as a rule, but the boy's very young voice had startled me. It had come through to me as a real voice will sound sometimes through a dream, almost waking you, but now it had stopped, and the dream was thick round me again, and I laid him down, covered his face with the brown blanket, and called two other old ones.

"Put this one in the corridor to make more room here," I

said; and I saw them lift him up. When they had taken him away, the stretcher bearers who had been waiting brought the blind one and put him down in the cleared space. They had to come round to the end of the front row and down between the row of feet and row of heads; they had to be very careful where they stepped; they had to lower the stretcher cautiously so as not to jostle the men on either side (there was just room), but these paid no attention. None of the men lying packed together on the floor noticed each other in this curious dream-place.

I had watched this out of the corner of my eye, busy with something that was not very like a man. The limbs seemed to be held together only by the strong stuff of the uniform. The head was unrecognisable. It was a monstrous thing, and a dreadful rattling sound came from it. I looked up and saw the chief surgeon standing over me. I don't know how he got there. His small shrunken face was wet and white; his eyes were brilliant and feverish; his incredible hands that saved so many men so exquisitely, so quickly, were in the pockets of his white coat.

"Give him morphine," he said, "a double dose. As much as you like." He pulled a cigarette out of his pocket. "In cases like this, if I am not about, give morphine; enough, you understand." Then he vanished like a ghost. He went back to his operating room, a small white figure with round shoulders, a magician, who performed miracles with knives. He went away through the dream.

I gave the morphine, then crawled over and looked at the

blind man's ticket. I did not know, of course, that he was blind until I read his ticket. A large round white helmet covered the top half of his head and face; only his nostrils and mouth and chin were uncovered. The surgeon in the dressing station behind the trenches had written on his ticket, "Shot through the eyes. Blind."

Did he know? I asked myself. No, he couldn't know yet. He would still be wondering, waiting, hoping, down there in that deep, dark silence of his, in his own dark personal world. He didn't know he was blind; no one would have told him. I felt his pulse. It was strong and steady. He was a long, thin man, but his body was not very cold and the pale lower half of his clear-cut face was not very pale. There was something beautiful about him. In his case there was no hurry, no necessity to rush him through to the operating room. There was plenty of time. He would always be blind.

One of the orderlies was going up and down with hot tea in a bucket. I beckoned to him.

I said to the blind one: "Here is a drink." He didn't hear me, so I said it more loudly against the bandage, and helped him lift his head, and held the tin cup to his mouth below the thick edge of the bandage. I did not think then of what was hidden under the bandage. I think of it now. Another head case across the hut had thrown off his blanket and risen from his stretcher. He was standing stark naked except for his head bandage, in the middle of the hut, and was haranguing the crowd in a loud voice with the gestures of a political orator. But the crowd, ly-

ing on the floor, paid no attention to him. They did not notice
him. I called to Gustave and Pierre to go to him.

The blind man said to me: "Thank you, sister, you are very
kind. That is good. I thank you." He had a beautiful voice. I noticed the great courtesy of his speech. But they were all courte-
ous. Their courtesy when they died, their reluctance to cause
me any trouble by dying or suffering, was one of the things it
didn't do to think about.

Then I left him, and presently forgot that he was there waiting in the second row of stretchers on the left side of the long
crowded floor.

Gustave and Pierre had got the naked orator back on to his
stretcher and were wrapping him up again in his blankets. I let
them deal with him and went back to my kitchen at the other
end of the hut, where my syringes and hypodermic needles
were boiling in saucepans. I had received by post that same
morning a dozen beautiful new platinum needles. I was very
pleased with them. I said to one of the dressers as I fixed a
needle on my syringe and held it up, squirting the liquid
through it: "Look. I've some lovely new needles." He said:
"Come and help me a moment. Just cut this bandage, please."
I went over to his dressing-table. He darted off to a voice that
was shrieking somewhere. There was a man stretched on the
table. His brain came off in my hands when I lifted the bandage from his head.

When the dresser came back I said: "His brain came off on
the bandage."

"Where have you put it?"

"I put it in the pail under the table."

"It's only one half of his brain," he said, looking into the man's skull. "The rest is here."

I left him to finish the dressing and went about my own business. I had much to do.

It was my business to sort out the wounded as they were brought in from the ambulances and to keep them from dying before they got to the operating rooms: it was my business to sort out the nearly dying from the dying. I was there to sort them out and tell how fast life was ebbing from them. Life was leaking away from all of them; but with some there was no hurry, with others it was a case of minutes. It was my business to create a counter-wave of life, to create the flow against the ebb. It was like a tug of war with the tide. The ebb of life was cold. When life was ebbing the man was cold; when it began to flow back, he grew warm. It was all, you see, like a dream. The dying men on the floor were drowned men cast up on the beach, and there was the ebb of life pouring away over them, sucking them away, an invisible tide; and my old orderlies, like old sea-salts out of a lifeboat, were working to save them. I had to watch, to see if they were slipping, being dragged away. If a man were slipping quickly, being sucked down rapidly, I sent runners to the operating rooms. There were six operating rooms on either side of my hut. Medical students in white coats hurried back and forth along the covered corridors between us. It was my business to know which of the wounded could wait and which could not. I had to decide for myself.

Blind

There was no one to tell me. If I made any mistakes, some would die on their stretchers on the floor under my eyes who need not have died. I didn't worry. I didn't think. I was too busy, too absorbed in what I was doing. I had to judge from what was written on their tickets and from the way they looked and the way they felt to my hand. My hand could tell of itself one kind of cold from another. They were all half-frozen when they arrived, but the chill of their icy flesh wasn't the same as the cold inside them when life was almost ebbed away. My hands could instantly tell the difference between the cold of the harsh bitter night and the stealthy cold of death. Then there was another thing, a small fluttering thing. I didn't think about it or count it. My fingers felt it. I was in a dream, led this way and that by my acute eyes and hands that did many things, and seemed to know what to do.

Sometimes there was no time to read the ticket or touch the pulse. The door kept opening and shutting to let in the stretcher-bearers whatever I was doing. I could not watch when I was giving piqûres; but, standing by my table filling a syringe, I could look down over the rough forms that covered the floor and pick out at a distance this one and that one. I had been doing this for two years, and had learned to read the signs. I could tell from the way they twitched, from the peculiar shade of a pallid face, from the look of tight pinched-in nostrils, and in other ways which I could not have explained, that this or that one was slipping over the edge of the beach of life. Then I would go quickly with my long saline needles, or short thick camphor oil needles, and send one of the old ones hurrying along the corridor to the operating rooms. But sometimes there was no need to hurry; sometimes I was too late; with some there was no longer any question of the ebb and flow of life and death; there was nothing to do.

The hospital throbbed and hummed that night like a dynamo. The operating rooms were ablaze; twelve surgical équipes were at work; boilers steamed and whistled; nurses hurried in and out of the sterilizing rooms carrying big shining metal boxes and enamelled trays; feet were running, slower feet shuffling. The hospital was going full steam ahead. I had a sense of great power, exhilaration and excitement. A loud wind was howling. It was throwing itself like a pack of wolves against the flimsy wooden walls, and the guns were growling. Their voices were dying away. I thought of them as a pack of beaten dogs, slinking away across the dark waste where the dead were lying and the wounded who had not yet been picked up, their only cover the windy blanket of the bitter November night.

And I was happy. It seemed to me that the crazy crowded bright hot shelter was a beautiful place. I thought, "This is the second battlefield. The battle now is going on over the helpless bodies of these men. It is we who are doing the fighting now, with their real enemies." And I thought of the chief surgeon, the wizard working like lightning through the night, and all the others wielding their flashing knives against the invisible enemy. The wounded had begun to arrive at noon. It was now past midnight, and the door kept opening and shutting to let in the stretcher-bearers, and the ambulances kept lurching in at the gate. Lanterns were moving through the windy dark, from shed to shed. The nurses were out there in the scattered huts, putting the men to bed when they came over the dark ground, asleep, from the operating rooms. They would wake up in clean warm beds—those who did wake up.

"We will send you the dying, the desperate, the moribund," the Inspector-General had said. "You must expect a thirty per cent. mortality." So we had got ready for it; we had organised to dispute that figure.

We had built brick ovens, four of them, down the centre of the hut, and on top of these, galvanised iron cauldrons of boiling water were steaming. We had driven nails all the way down the wooden posts that held up the roof and festooned the posts with red rubber hot-water bottles. In the corner near to my kitchen we had partitioned off a cubicle, where we built a light bed, a rough wooden frame lined with electric light bulbs, where a man could be cooked back to life again. My own kitchen was an arrangement of shelves for saucepans and syringes and needles of different sizes, and cardboard boxes full of ampoules of camphor oil and strychnine and caffeine and morphine, and large ampoules of sterilized salt and water, and dozens of beautiful sharp shining needles were always on the boil.

It wasn't much to look at, this reception hut. It was about as attractive as a goods yard in a railway station, but we were very proud of it, my old ones and I. We had got it ready, and it was good enough for us. We could revive the cold dead there; snatch back the men who were slipping over the edge; hoist them out of the dark abyss into life again. And because our mortality at the end of three months was only nineteen per cent., not thirty, well it was the most beautiful place in the world to me and my old grizzled Pépères, Gaston and Pierre and Leroux and the others were to me like shining archangels. But I didn't think about this. I think of it now. I only knew it then, and was happy. Yes, I was happy there.

Looking back, I do not understand that woman—myself—standing in that confused goods yard filled with bundles of broken human flesh. The place by one o'clock in the morning was a shambles. The air was thick with steaming sweat, with the effluvia of mud, dirt, blood. The men lay in their stiff uniforms that were caked with mud and dried blood, their great boots on their feet; stained bandages showing where a trouser leg or a sleeve had been cut away. Their faces gleamed faintly, with a faint phosphorescence. Some who could not breathe lying down were propped up on their stretchers against the wall, but most were prone on their backs, staring at the steep iron roof.

The old orderlies moved from one stretcher to another, carefully, among the piles of clothing, boots and blood-soaked bandages—careful not to step on a hand or a sprawling twisted foot. They carried zinc pails of hot water and slabs of yellow soap and scrubbing brushes. They gathered up the heaps of clothing, and made little bundles of the small things out of pockets, or knelt humbly, washing the big yellow stinking feet that protruded from under the brown blankets. It was the business of these old ones to undress the wounded, wash them, wrap them in blankets, and put hot-water bottles at their feet and sides. It was a difficult business peeling the stiff uniform

Blind

from a man whose hip or shoulder was fractured, but the old ones were careful. Their big peasant hands were gentle—very, very gentle and careful. They handled the wounded men as if they were children. Now, looking back, I see their rough powerful visages, their shaggy eyebrows, their big clumsy, gentle hands. I see them go down on their stiff knees; I hear their shuffling feet and their soft gruff voices answering the voices of the wounded, who are calling to them for drinks, or to God for mercy.

The old ones had orders from the commandant not to cut the good cloth of the uniforms if they could help it, but they had orders from me not to hurt the men, and they obeyed me. They slit up the heavy trousers and slashed across the stiff tunics with long scissors, and pulled very slowly, very carefully at the heavy boots, and the wounded men did not groan or cry out very much. They were mostly very quiet. When they did cry out they usually apologised for the annoyance of their agony. Only now and then a wind of pain would sweep over the floor, tossing the legs and arms, then subside again.

I think that woman, myself, must have been in a trance, or under some horrid spell. Her feet are lumps of fire, her face is clammy, her apron is splashed with blood; but she moves ceaselessly about with bright burning eyes and handles the dreadful wreckage of men as if in a dream. She does not seem to notice the wounds or the blood. Her eyes seem to be watching something that comes and goes and darts in and out among the prone bodies. Her eyes and her hands and her ears are alert, intent on the unseen thing that scurries and hides and jumps out of the corner on to the face of a man when she's not looking. But quick, something makes her turn. Quick, she is over there, on her knees fighting the thing off, driving it away, and now it's got another victim. It's like a dreadful game of hide and seek among the wounded. All her faculties are intent on it. The other things that are going on, she deals with automatically.

There is a constant coming and going. Medical students run in and out.

"What have you got ready?"

"I've got three knees, two spines, five abdomens, twelve heads. Here's a lung case—hæmorrhage. He can't wait." She is binding the man's chest; she doesn't look up.

"Send him along."

"Pierre! Gaston! Call the stretcher-bearers to take the lung to Monsieur D——." She fastens the tight bandage, tucks the blanket quickly round the thin shoulders. The old men lift him. She hurries back to her saucepans to get a new needle.

A surgeon appears.

"Where's that knee of mine? I left it in the saucepan on the window ledge. I had boiled it up for an experiment."

"One of the orderlies must have taken it," she says, putting her old needle on to boil.

"Good God! Did he mistake it?"

"Jean, did you take a saucepan you found on the window-sill?"

"Yes, sister, I took it. I thought it was for the casse-croûte; it looked like a ragout of mouton. I have it here."

Blind

"Well, it was lucky he didn't eat it. It was a knee I had cut out, you know."

It is time for the old ones' casse-croûte. It is after one o'clock. At one o'clock the orderlies have cups of coffee and chunks of bread and meat. They eat their supper gathered round the stoves where the iron cauldrons are boiling. The surgeons and the sisters attached to the operating rooms are drinking coffee too in the sterilizing rooms. I do not want any supper. I am not hungry. I am not tired. I am busy. My eyes are busy and my fingers. I am conscious of nothing about myself but my eyes, hands and feet. My feet are a nuisance, they are swollen, hurting lumps, but my fingers are perfectly satisfactory. They are expert in the handling of frail glass ampoules and syringes and needles. I go from one man to another jabbing the sharp needles into their sides, rubbing their skins with iodine, and each time I pick my way back across their bodies to fetch a fresh needle I scan the surface of the floor where the men are spread like a carpet, for signs, for my special secret signals of death.

"Aha! I'll catch you out again." Quick, to that one. That jerking! That sudden livid hue spreading over his form. "Quick, Emile! Pierre!" I have lifted the blanket. The blood is pouring out on the floor under the stretcher. "Get the tourniquet. Hold his leg up. Now then, tight—tighter. Now call the stretcher bearers."

Someone near is having a fit. Is it epilepsy? I don't know. His mouth is frothy. His eyes are rolling. He tries to fling himself on the floor. He falls with a thud across his neighbour, who does not notice. The man just beyond propped up against the wall, watches as if from a great distance. He has a gentle patient face; this spectacle does not concern him.

The door keeps opening and shutting to let in the stretcher-bearers. The wounded are carried in at the end door and are carried out to the operating rooms at either side. The sergeant is counting the treasures out of a dead man's pockets. He is tying his little things, his letters and briquet, etc., up in a handkerchief. Some of the old ones are munching their bread and meat in the centre of the hut under the electric light. The others are busy with their pails and scissors. They shuffle about, kneeling, scrubbing, filling hot-water bottles. I see it all through a mist. It is misty but eternal. It is a scene in eternity, in some strange dream-hell where I am glad to be employed, where I belong, where I am happy. How crowded together we are here. How close we are in this nightmare. The wounded are packed into this place like sardines, and we are so close to them, my old ones and I. I've never been so close before to human beings. We are locked together, the old ones and I, and the wounded men; we are bound together. We all feel it. We all know it. The same thing is throbbing in us, the single thing, the one life. We are one body, suffering and bleeding. It is a kind of bliss to me to feel this. I am a little delirious, but my head is cool enough, it seems to me.

"No, not that one. He can wait. Take the next one to Monsieur D——, and this one to Monsieur Guy, and this one to Monsieur Robert. We will put this one on the electric-light bed; he has no pulse. More hot-water bottles here, Gaston.

Blind

"Do you feel cold, mon vieux?"

"Yes, I think so, but pray do not trouble."

I go with him into the little cubicle, turn on the light bulbs, leave him to cook there; and as I come out again to face the strange heaving dream, I suddenly hear a voice calling me, a new far-away hollow voice.

"Sister! My sister! Where are you?"

I am startled. It sounds so far away, so hollow and so sweet. It sounds like a bell high up in the mountains. I do not know where it comes from. I look down over the rows of men lying on their backs, one close to the other, packed together on the floor, and I cannot tell where the voice comes from. Then I hear it again.

"Sister! Oh, my sister, where are you?"

A lost voice. The voice of a lost man, wandering in the mountains, in the night. It is the blind man calling. I had forgotten him. I had forgotten that he was there. He could wait. The others could not wait. So I had left him and forgotten him.

Something in his voice made me run, made my heart miss a beat. I ran down the centre alley way, round and up again, between the two rows, quickly, carefully stepping across to him over the stretchers that separated us. He was in the second row. I could just squeeze through to him.

"I am coming," I called to him. "I am coming."

I knelt beside him. "I am here," I said; but he lay quite still on his back; he didn't move at all; he hadn't heard me. So I took his hand and put my mouth close to his bandaged head and called to him with desperate entreaty.

"I am here. What is it? What is the matter?"

He didn't move even then, but he gave a long shuddering sigh of relief.

"I thought I had been abandoned here, all alone," he said softly in his far-away voice.

I seemed to awake then. I looked round me and began to tremble, as one would tremble if one awoke with one's head over the edge of a precipice. I saw the wounded packed round us, hemming us in. I saw his comrades, thick round him, and the old ones shuffling about, working and munching their hunks of bread, and the door opening to let in the stretcher bearers. The light poured down on the rows of faces. They gleamed faintly. Four hundred faces were staring up at the roof, side by side. The blind man didn't know. He thought he was alone, out in the dark. That was the precipice, that reality.

"You are not alone," I lied. "There are many of your comrades here, and I am here, and there are doctors and nurses. You are with friends here, not alone."

"I thought," he murmured in that far-away voice, "that you had gone away and forgotten me, and that I was abandoned here alone."

My body rattled and jerked like a machine out of order. I was awake now, and I seemed to be breaking to pieces.

"No," I managed to lie again. "I had not forgotten you, nor left you alone." And I looked down again at the visible half of his face and saw that his lips were smiling.

At that I fled from him. I ran down the long, dreadful hut

and hid behind my screen and cowered, sobbing, in a corner, hiding my face.

The old ones were very troubled. They didn't know what to do. Presently I heard them whispering:

"She is tired," one said.

"Yes, she is tired."

"She should go off to bed," another said.

"We will manage somehow without her," they said.

Then one of them timidly stuck a grizzled head round the corner of the screen. He held his tin cup in his hands. It was full of hot coffee. He held it out, offering it to me. He didn't know of anything else that he could do for me.